The History of Whiskey

Also by Robin Robinson

*The Complete Whiskey Course:
A Comprehensive Tasting School in
Ten Classes*

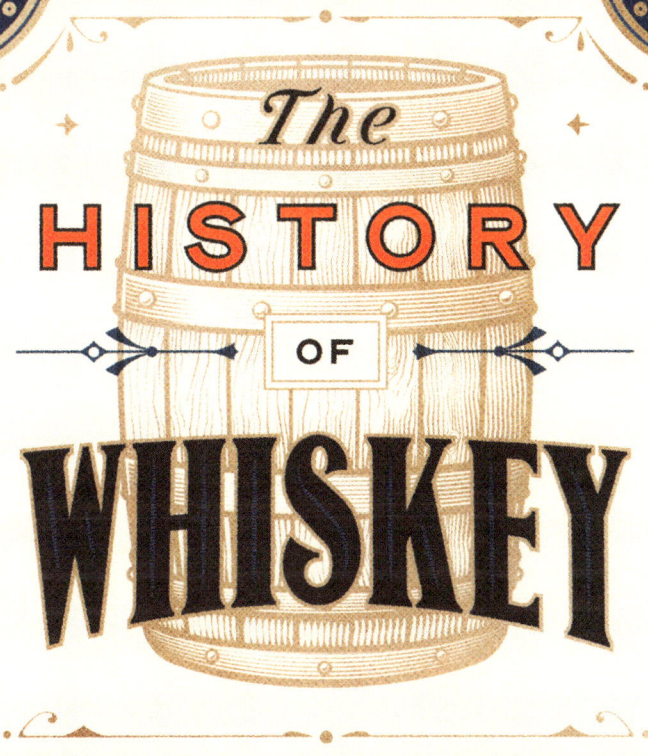

The HISTORY OF WHISKEY

IN 100 BOTTLES, BARRELS, AND MORE

✦ ROBIN ROBINSON ✦

Countryman Press

An Imprint of W. W. Norton & Company
Independent Publishers Since 1923

Copyright © 2025 by Robin Robinson

All rights reserved
Printed in Malaysia
First Edition

For information about permission to reproduce selections from this book, write to
Permissions, Countryman Press, 500 Fifth Avenue, New York, NY 10110

For information about special discounts for bulk purchases, please contact
W. W. Norton Special Sales at specialsales@wwnorton.com or 800-233-4830

Manufacturing through Imago
Book design by Raphael Geroni
Production manager: Devon Zahn

Countryman Press
www.countrymanpress.com

An imprint of W. W. Norton & Company, Inc.
500 Fifth Avenue, New York, NY 10110
www.wwnorton.com

978-1-68268-910-3

1 2 3 4 5 6 7 8 9 0

*To Amy and Rose,
our history of
love, support, and
encouragement for each
other continues to write
our future together.*

CONTENTS

Introduction ◆ x

NEOLITHIC PERIOD
Cucurbit ◆ 2

IRON AGE
Wooden Barrel ◆ 6

CLASSICAL ANTIQUITY
Alembic ◆ 10
Mary's Bath ◆ 12
Hydrometer ◆ 14

MIDDLE AGES
Old Jenever ◆ 18
Cloth of Armagnac ◆ 20

RENAISSANCE
Lindores Abbey ◆ 24

BAROQUE ERA
Smugglers' Companions ◆ 28
Grande Chartreuse ◆ 30
Charter of Coleraine ◆ 32
Quaich ◆ 34
The First Families of Whisky ◆ 36
A Pot of Poitín ◆ 37
The Taxman Cometh ◆ 40
Rumbullion to Rye ◆ 42
Ryes of the Mennonites ◆ 44

INDUSTRIAL AGE

Worm Tub ◆ 48
Cumberland Gap ◆ 50
Bow Street Distillery ◆ 52
The Golden Triangle ◆ 54
The Harbormaster ◆ 56
All the President's Whiskey ◆ 58
Old Overholts ◆ 60
Walker's Grocer's Shop ◆ 62
Spirit Safe ◆ 64
Beam's Old Tub ◆ 66
Flagging the Cardhu ◆ 67
Cameronbridge ◆ 69
Smith's Glenlivet ◆ 70
Charcoal Filtration ◆ 72
Crow's Sour Mash ◆ 74
Coffey Still ◆ 76
Usher in the Blends ◆ 78
Molson Distillery ◆ 79

VICTORIAN ERA

"Men into Swine" ◆ 82
The Booz Log Cabin Decanter ◆ 84
Cadenhead's Independent Bottling ◆ 86
Nelson's Green Brier Tennessee Whiskey ◆ 88
Uncle Nearest and Jack Daniel ◆ 89
Gooderham, Worts, and Canadian Industrialization ◆ 92
Vat 69 ◆ 94
Walkerville ◆ 95
The Whiskey Ring, PACs Americana ◆ 98
Golden Wedding Partners ◆ 100
Prescription in a Bottle ◆ 102
Bourbon Pompeii ◆ 104
Whiskey as Big Business ◆ 106

MACHINE AGE

Seagram's Charmed Life ◆ 112

The Whiskey Trust ◆ 113

Saladin Box ◆ 115

Ashley's Bottle Machine ◆ 117

Dewar's Labels ◆ 119

Taylor versus Stagg ◆ 121

Baby Power ◆ 122

Corry's Hand-Blown Bottles ◆ 124

Takamine and the Koji Process ◆ 125

Bullitts Behind Your Best Bourbon ◆ 128

20TH CENTURY

Duffy's Cure and the Fall of Patent Medicines ◆ 132

Hotaling's Warehouse ◆ 134

Maryland Rye ◆ 136

Sweating Barrels ◆ 137

Teacher's Self-Opening Bottle ◆ 140

Hatch's Navy ◆ 141

The Macallan 1928: The World's Rarest Whisky? ◆ 143

Shirofuda ◆ 144

The Father and Mother of Japanese Whisky ◆ 146

Kakubin ◆ 147

Crown Royal ◆ 149

Smirnoff's White "Whiskey" ◆ 152

Rise of Indian Whisky ◆ 153

COLD WAR

Knappogue Castle ◆ 158
Shirakawa of the Golden Age ◆ 160
The Ceramic Sizzle ◆ 162
Birth of the Single Malt ◆ 164
The Nadir of Irish Whiskey ◆ 166
The Hidden Power of Irish Whiskey ◆ 168
Pappy Van Winkle's Family Reserve ◆ 170
Light Whiskey ◆ 172
Seagram's Legacy ◆ 174
Cooley's Challenge ◆ 176
The Birth of French Whisky ◆ 178

REBIRTH AT CENTURY'S END

The New Age of American Whiskey ◆ 182
Single Malts Come to America ◆ 183
Rediscovery of Grain Whiskies ◆ 185
A Tale of Talisker ◆ 186
Three-Chamber Still ◆ 188

DIGITAL AGE

Bruichladdich Distillery ◆ 192
Five Strains for Four Roses ◆ 194
The Einstein of Whisky ◆ 196
Wales Gets Back in the Game ◆ 197
Farm Distilleries Return to Scotland ◆ 199
The Legend of Popcorn Sutton ◆ 200
The Quest of Shackleton's Whisky ◆ 202
I Want My MGP ◆ 204
Liquid Genealogy ◆ 205
Angel's Envy, a Bourbon Ex-Port ◆ 207
A Glass of Milk ◆ 208
Japanese Straight Flush ◆ 210
Amphorae of Athyr ◆ 212

Acknowledgments ◆ 215
Bibliography ◆ 217
Credits ◆ 223
Index ◆ 225

INTRODUCTION

Some whiskey drinkers contentedly open a bottle and drink with friends in camaraderie or loved ones in celebration. For them, whiskey serves as a social lubricant that connects us, with more flavor than vodka and more punch than beer. They ask no more of it than to be "smooth" and maybe have a good story. It follows a certain mythology of place from ages past: the rugged Highlands of Scotland, the damp streets of Dublin, the mountain hollows of Kentucky, or the wide plains of the American West. They drink it as a dream of liquid adventure.

Others look deep into the label, past the font and through the graphics. They swim through the long journey of the brown water: from its origin as grain, through its transmutation by yeast to bubbling beer, to its distillation into spirit. They note the farmer's soil, the brewer's mash tun, the distiller's pot, and even the humidity of the warehouse. They observe the whiskey's place in history and follow the crazy, winding road that it traveled through during its technological advances, Prohibition, plant closings, untimely deaths, and corporate mergers. Each sip offers a specificity of time and place, of persons real and imagined, all converging in the glass, then past the lips and over the tongue.

I've enjoyed drams with both camps, the new enthusiast and the veteran connoisseur. And each was with me as I contemplated writing this history of whiskey, one perched on each shoulder, balancing me between historical detail and telling a good story. My love and respect for history runs deep, but I'm not a professional historian. When done badly, historiography (the technical term) can mire even eager readers in a bog of sluggish facts and mind-numbing minutiae. On the other hand, the whiskey industry suffers from a glut of free-form stories written by lazy marketers, so-called journalists, and cavalier bloggers who never let the truth or a lack of compelling evidence get in the way of a good yarn. Their imaginations soar into the atmosphere as facts splat gracelessly to the ground.

I'm a storyteller. It's what I do and always have done. A story grounded in truth resonates better than one pulled from thin air. Stories move us, but facts ground us. So my goal with this book has been to move slowly enough to get it right and

Barrels, hoops, and staves.

quickly enough to keep it interesting. Writing lives-of-the-saints profiles (hagiography, another technical term) of people, brands, or companies doesn't interest me, either. I work in the spirits industry, so I kind of know where the skeletons, and real stories, lie.

Some facts, stories, people, brands, and companies don't appear in the book because what mattered most or captured my imagination went a different way, and (as my editor reminds me) every book has a target word count. Until the 21st century, no one cared about whiskey's history, and the recent flood of information is full of contradictions and open to interpretations. In some cases, that information has become a trade secret meriting protection at all costs. In cases of conjecture, extrapolations, and other uncertainties, the bibliography lists a whole library of articles, books, and other resources that I consulted at length. If three or more neutral, independent authorities point to the same information, the truth probably lies in that direction.

The history of whiskey consists of many stories, each with its own arc, all joined together, like staves of a barrel held in place by hoops. Rolling with that metaphor, this book has the following ten main hoops, or themes, that help hold it all together.

◆ **FOR MOST OF THE TIME THAT WE'VE BEEN DRINKING HARD ALCOHOL, WE'VE CONSUMED IT FOR ITS CURATIVE POWERS, TREATING IT AS MEDICINE**. In the Middle Ages, European alchemists transformed herbal mixtures made with distilled spirits to create our first of ideas of the "water of life" or aqua vitae, a curative for all ailments. During the Hundred Years' War, the health of King Charles II of Navarre was failing, so his physician instructed attendants to wrap the king in brandy-soaked linen (page 20), which famously caught fire and burned him alive. James E. Pepper advertised that more than "30,000 physicians have tested, prescribed and dispensed" his bourbon "in their clinical work" (page 103). In 1920, when the American Prohibition went into effect, the federal government licensed six distilleries to make and sell medicinal whiskey (page 102). Even now, people crack wise about its antiseptic properties while making hot toddies to weather illness.

◆ **A SPIRITED TRINITY GOVERNS THE WHOLE OPERATION: FARMER, DISTILLER, AND TAX COLLECTOR**. The farmer contributes excess grain. The distiller concentrates it into a powerful liquid. The taxman takes a cut, which, without fail, prompts the distiller—and sometimes the farmer—to innovate. English Parliament imposed a malt tax in Ireland in 1697, which led to a new style of poitín (page 40). In 1713, a similar tax triggered riots in Scotland and caused a rise in illegal stills in the Highlands. During the American Civil War, President Abraham Lincoln levied a tax on whiskey that, afterward, served as the foundation for a brazen system of corruption that foreshadowed the organized lawlessness of Prohibition (page 98).

◆ **FAMILY TIES MAKE A DIFFERENCE**. The Haigs and the Steins established the world's first distilling dynasties (page 36), and one of their mutual descendants married into the Jameson family, which established its own empire (page 52). In America, the Beam family has achieved similar fame in the marketplace (page 62). Even today, liquid genealogy continues breathing new life into the industry. In 2011, Cyrus Kehyari got back into the family business (Hughes Bros. Distillers), taking inspiration as a fourth-great-grandson of Michael Hughes, who left County Carlow and set up a still in Bedford, Pennsylvania (page 206).

In 2019, Charles and Andrew Nelson did the same after a butcher near where they grew up casually mentioned their thrice-great-grandfather's old distilling facility across the street (page 88).

◆ **THE PURSUIT OF PERFECTION AND PROFIT DRIVES INNOVATION.** In 1830, Aeneas Coffey, a taxman, adapted prior designs to create the precursor to the modern column still (page 76). In 1854, William Sanderson tested his blended whisky in Scotland in a variety of used barrels, leading to the eventual popularity of using ex-sherry barrels (page 94). In the 1880s, Charles Saladin perfected a mechanized malting trench (page 115). In 1886, H. M. Ashley created the small-mouth bottle that we use today (page 117). In 1891, the head of the Whiskey Trust brought Jokichi Takamine from Japan to Illinois to use his koji process to save money and increase yield (page 125).

◆ **QUALITY CONTROL ALWAYS WINS.** In the 1820s, James Crow formalized the sour mash process to fend off bacterial contamination and maintain consistency between batches (page 74). The Bottled in Bond Act of 1897 established legal definitions, preventing unscrupulous rectifiers from cutting whiskey with tea, prune juice, neutral grain spirits, and even kerosene (page 128). Later in the 20th century, Samuel Bronfman, head of Seagram, instituted meticulous quality control across all aspects of the business. His influence reaches into practically every bottle made today and helped make his company the largest beverage giant of its time (page 174).

◆ **NEVER UNDERESTIMATE THE POWER OF TEMPERANCE.** In Australia, excessive drinking met with equally excessive restrictions (page 82) almost a century before the same fate befell America. The growing temperance movement stateside prompted Hiram Walker, a Massachusetts native and Detroit transplant, to look across the water to Canada, where he later made Canadian Club whisky, beloved by British monarchs from Victoria to Elizabeth II (page 95). When America went dry in 1920, the Bourbon industry nearly flatlined, allowing Canada to strengthen and consolidate its place in world production (page 112).

◆ **IT ALL BECOMES A SHELL GAME.** Created in 1868, Golden Wedding Rye has passed through an astonishing number of iterations and owners, including Schenley, Guinness, Diageo, and now Sazerac (page 100). The corporatization of the whiskey business gained critical mass in the 1870s, with companies swallowing and divesting one another ever faster (page 92). Borrowing strategies from the oil barons of the age, Joseph Greenhut built the Whiskey Trust in the 1880s and 1890s, which forcibly consolidated 65 distilleries and more than 70 industrial alcohol plants before the government dissolved the monopoly (page 113). But not all the shells have dark endings. In the 1930s and 1940s, Samuel Bronfman of Seagram bought Kentucky distilleries that had gone defunct during Prohibition, preserving their historic mash bills, yeast strains, and methods (page 194). In 1966, the heads of Jameson, Powers, and Cork Distillers convened to create Irish Distillers Ltd, which French conglomerate Pernod Ricard eventually acquired, and for a time, Bushmills in Northern Ireland, saving the entire category of Irish whiskey from going under (page 166).

◆ **THERE'S ROOM AT THE TABLE FOR EVERYONE.** If you're doing something new, different, or good, drinkers will pay attention. In Japan, Shinjiro Torii and Masataka Taketsuru led the charge in the 1910s and 1920s, re-creating high-quality Scotch whisky in their country and founding their own companies that eventually became Suntory and Nikka (page 144). In Ireland, John Teeling broke the Irish Distillers monopoly by opening Cooley Distillery, the first independently owned facility in Ireland in more than 70 years, which revived Irish single malts and peated whiskeys (page 176). Producers in India (page 153), France (page 178), Israel (page 208), and Lebanon (page 212) are bringing their own unique and interesting takes on a truly global spirit to market.

◆ **MARKETING MATTERS.** In the 1880s and 1890s, Tommy Dewar weaponized bottle labels as billboards and knew the value of high-profile advertising (page 119). In 1939, when most Americans hadn't ever heard of vodka, Heublein Spirits of Connecticut acquired the Smirnoff brand, successfully bringing it to market as "white whiskey" (page 152). In the 1960s, when the whiskey industry worldwide was suffering, the Grant family rebranded Glenfiddich as a premium single malt, creating a new category that still dominates today (page 164).

◆ **NO ONE INVENTED WHISKEY.** It took a thousand years, by a thousand paths, to reach us. Only a handful of lucky, now legendary people made single-handed advances. In 1808, Jean-Baptiste Cellier-Blumenthal created a single-pass column still to separate sugar from beets, which Robert Stein patented for whisky in 1826 and Aeneas Coffey perfected in 1830. In 1819, James Fox received a patent for the spirit safe (page 64). In 1853, James Riley and William Allen modified Coffey's still design to distill rosin oil, which the Gooderhams adapted back to make whiskey distillation more efficient (page 92). In 1913, William Bergius, great-grandson of whiskey maker William Teacher, patented the resealable bottle (page 140). They all stood on the shoulders of everyone who came before them.

The history of whiskey traveled a crooked road for thousands of miles over many millennia. Whiskey was witness to, and perhaps a catalyst to innovation and advancement of the human race and the one hundred objects listed here are mere portals into the imagination of our ancestors. So pour a dram of your favorite brand and join me on the journey.

A NOTE ON SPELLING

The spelling of whiskey is its own controversy. Today, Irish and the majority of American whiskeys insert the "e" in whiskey, while Scotch, Japanese, and Canadian whiskies, and those from the rest of the world, have kept the historic "whisky" spelling. For general usage, we'll use the American spelling, and when referencing the products of other countries, we'll revert to the appropriate version.

NEOLITHIC PERIOD

CUCURBIT

IN THE BEGINNING WAS THE POT. IN PREHISTORY, MORE THAN 25,000 years ago, a pot consisted of a depression in a rock formation deep enough to hold rainwater or to accommodate mashing with a stick; an animal skin suspended on a wooden frame; or a hollowed-out gourd. Its structure held vegetation, water, or rocks infused with minerals, and in some cases blood. In time, the pot took its shape using other materials: wood, clay, ceramics, bronze, or copper. In these vessels, one element combined with another—perhaps mashed tubers, fat from the last kill, available herbs—before heat cooked the mixture or the sun dried it. These disparate ingredients formed a new mass, a type of stew, its integrated flavors pleasing and nutritious, simple and functional.

The peoples of Sumer, Ancient Egypt, and Assyria realized that cooking in a heatproof pot that approximated a gourd could serve a higher purpose. The Latin word for gourd, *cucurbita,* now describes a genus in the gourd family that includes melons, pumpkins, and other squash. In a pot made from a gourd, they could reduce roots, vines, seeds, and fruit to create an elixir of health, be it a salve to ward off disease or a fumigation to cleanse bad air. This new use of the vessel not for cooking but for transforming elements into something new serves as our starting point. The idea of whiskey, not yet whiskey itself, started with this crude and ancient pot.

As history advances from the Macedonian Empire, through the Romanized world, to the caliphates of Islam, those ritual elixirs grew more central to civilization. Holy men and other wielders of earthly power took this pot in hand to unlock natural phenomena and summon the supernatural. In service to their needs, they standardized the pot's shape, dimensions, and materials throughout. It has traveled through tens of thousands of years and survived thousands of tweaks and innovations in the name of efficiency. Today, we see the cucurbit as the bottom part of a modern distilling device, a flowering husk that can hold liquid and from which something new will bloom.

But it's still just a pot that looks like a gourd.

Neolithic Period

IRON AGE

WOODEN BARREL

THIS CIRCLE OF PERFECTION, A FEAT OF ANCIENT TECHNOLOGY, HAS lasted longer than several Chinese dynasties, the Roman Empire, and the reign of the Black Death. Only fire, the wheel, and metallurgy have eclipsed it, and all three are necessary for its construction. Invented by the Celts and perfected by the Romans, the barrel was the ideal lightweight, water-tight conveyor of liquids and solids, from rocks to fish, from whale oil to wine, and, of course, whiskey.

Over the centuries, it became a unit of measure and its dimensions set the regulations of trade and taxation, as well as the mode of transport and delivery. Distilleries filled barrels with whiskey and transported them to points of sale for dispersal: taverns, shops, or for personal use. The barrel head displayed the maker's mark. At the shop or tavern, drinkers filled their personal containers and went on their way, but the name of the whiskey maker stayed at the bar, a folly that many of us immediately recognize today. At the same time, most tavern owners adulterated the contents of the barrel at the bar, rectifying it with modifiers: wine or juice to change the taste, kerosene or solvent to give it more punch, or water to stretch it. In the movie, *Gangs of New York* by Martin Scorsese, based on the book by Herbert Asbury, published in 1928 and set in the mid-1800s, a key scene in a rowdy bar demonstrates the barrel's misuse, with a common tavern practice since the early 1800s called "all sorts." During a wild night of revelry, a barrel sits at the bar bearing a sign with those words. A patron is charged a coin to sip from an attached hose while the bartender empties the remains of all the discarded bar drinks, the dregs, through a funnel in its top.

Prior to the advent of shipping in bottles, Spanish bodegas delivered sherry to the docks of the British Isles in heavy transport casks. The boat journey and time at the ports allowed the thick wooden staves to absorb the spirit's rich sweetness. Distillers and bonders prized those barrels, after use, for aging their whiskey, and in the late 1800s and early 1900s, those barrels set the flavor profiles of Scotch and Irish whiskey.

Need determined barrel size, from tiny firkins and rundlets used as individual containers to vast butts and pipes to hold solera-aged, fortified wines. Scottish

distillers favored the hogshead, in use since the 1400s, but the American wine industry standardized the 53-gallon barrel that is used by the American whiskey industry today to fit a rickhouse's open racks.

To mimic the darkness of imported brandies favored by the drinking elite in the 1700s and 1800s, new barrels in America often were charred inside to impart color to the clear corn and rye whiskeys that filled them up. As an unintended benefit, the resulting intensity of flavor greatly improved the taste and drinkability of whiskey.

Iron Age

CLASSICAL ANTIQUITY

ALEMBIC

MODERN DISTILLING PARLANCE REFERS TO THE POT STILL AS THE "alembic," a gourd-shaped container with a larger bottom that tapers to a narrow pipe at the top. From a technical perspective, the alembic refers only to the top part of the pot still, and it comes in a wide variety of shapes depending on whether a maker is distilling rose water, whiskey, rum, or something else. In the Gascony region of France, where Armagnac originates, distillers extend the definition to include an enclosed column with seven to nine plates that passes the alcohol vapor to a separate condenser.

The alembic holds the roots of chemistry and chemical engineering, and the idea is simple. As fermented mash boils in the bottom of the pot (the cucurbit), alcohol vapor collects as condensation inside the top of the pot. That condensation becomes brandy if from fruit mash, or whiskey if from grain. This process begins with the ancient Egyptians, and the Arabic world carries it through history to alchemists of the last thousand years. For all of them, the act of distillation represented a spiritual, holy experience, always called "the great work." Distillation synthesizes through separation, and it embodied the mortal separation from the immortal self. Alchemists such as Zosimos of Panopolis (circa 300 C.E., Egypt) and Albertus Magnus (circa 1200–1280, Holy Roman Empire) used the alembic, also known as the retort, to reunite various parts of the human psyche in a spiritual experience. The synthesis itself occurred in the alembic, where the pure "essence" reformed in a redeemed state of perfect harmony: "First we bring together, then we putrefy, we break down what has been putrefied, we purify the divided,

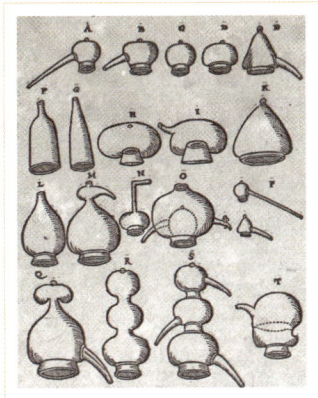

we unite the purified and harden it. In this way One is made from man and woman" (translated from the German of *The Little Book of the Philosopher's Stone,* 1778). Now you can see why we call it a spirit. The simple act of putting a cap on top of a pot to collect the condensation is an example of how slowly technology travels and when it arrives, it is filled with enormous importance and symbolic meaning. The alembic bore the roots of chemistry and engineering.

  Still makers of the modern age create a wide range of equipment for storage, brewing, and distilling, the best of them earning a reputation for the traditional hand-hammering of their copper stills to one of three basic shapes: ogee, lamp glass, and boil ball. They are finished with a sweeping swan neck, or lyne arm, at the top to conjure the most delicate aromas from the pot and reformulate them in the bottle that you enjoy with friends and family.

MARY'S BATH

AS WITH SO MUCH OF THE HISTORY OF SCIENCE AND INDUSTRY, WHICH includes distilling, the names of women often are missing. Stretching back to the Sumerian and Egyptian civilizations, priests and other men controlled most power structures. Moving through the Greek city-states and Muslim caliphates doesn't improve that situation. But throughout history, women not only watched the pot, but they also acted as compounders, tradespeople, and transporters. Victors armed with either a sword or pen write history, and women, as a group, had neither.

However, in this dark miasma appears one small reference to a woman who advanced distillation technology. Brilliant, essential, and overlooked, she was known as Mary the Jewess or Maria the Prophetess. Five centuries after her time, Zosimos of Panopolis, an Egyptian alchemist who chronicled the scientific thinking of the period, recorded her contribution to the field. Scholars interpreted *Jewess*, his descriptor of her, as "sister of Moses," and you may have one of her inventions in your kitchen today: the bain-marie (Mary's bath) or double boiler.

She lived in the first century of the common era and helped ancient chemistry move forward. Less concerned with the alchemical transmutation of life, she pursued practical applications of distillation and sublimation. Her *kerotakis* device fused together the cucurbit (bottom pot) and the alembic (top pot) with the tube (lyne arm) into a tight vacuum, or hermetic seal, that used water to heat a substance indirectly. In this way, her work had less to do with philosophy and more to do with chemical engineering. Distilling as we know it wouldn't have developed without this giant leap.

In the 21st century, her practical descendants have reclaimed a rightful place for women in the whiskey world. Rachel Barrie, Emma Walker, and Stephanie Macleod lead the way in Scotland. In America, Lisa Wicker, Andrea Wilson, and Heather Greene practice the arts of distilling and blending. Mary's avatar itself seems to have returned in the form of Nicole Austin. Trained as a chemical engineer and gifted with a remarkable palate, Austin has run several prestigious distilleries, including Kings County Distillery in Brooklyn, Tullamore DEW in Ireland, and Cascade Hollow in Tennessee. In the craft whiskey movement, her activism has placed her at the forefront of issues such as the rise of state guilds and excise tax reform

(commemorated by the bill number tattooed on her arm). Each of these remarkable people is creating new wisdom for future generations, ensuring that no woman has to wait another five hundred years for someone to discover her talents.

Classical Antiquity

HYDROMETER

ARCHIMEDES OF SYRACUSE (CIRCA 287–212 B.C.E.) REPORTEDLY SAT in a bathtub and noticed that the water rose as he submerged, prompting his "eureka" moment. He observed displacement, which helped him formulate what we call the Archimedes' principle, a fundamental law of physics. It allows for calculating the buoyancy of any floating object partially or fully immersed in a fluid. Its real-life applications help design boats and airships, determine the weight of precious metals, and proof your whiskey.

Archimedes's discovery eventually led to the hydrometer, a device that tells distillers exactly how much alcohol a spirit contains. It begins with Hypatia (circa 360–415 C.E.), a mathematician in fifth-century Alexandria, Egypt. She first described its basic shape and structure, which hasn't changed much since then: "a cylindrical tube which has the shape of a flute." Notches on the side enable measurement, and when placed in a solution, "you can count the notches at your ease to ascertain the weight of the water." When placed in low-density liquids, such as alcohol, the hydrometer sinks. This tool proved critical for the distiller, and it became the chief tool of his antagonist, the tax collector, who could determine the final strength of a spirit to gauge the proper tax burden.

But the hydrometer fell into a deep sleep of about a thousand years. During that time, the idea of "proof" developed as a test for alcohol strength. The test became a simple burn-or-no-burn binary: Soak a pellet of gunpowder in the liquid and try to ignite it. If it burned—or exploded, as often happened—the alcohol ranked as "above proof" and qualified for a higher tax rate. In the 1600s, the work of Francis Bacon, Robert Boyle, and other chemists introduced the idea of specific gravity, a ratio of the relative density of a substance. But of course, each country measured this density differently.

In 1824, the French developed a scale that set 100 percent water by volume as 0 proof and 100 percent alcohol by volume (ABV) as 100 proof. But in 1848, at the behest of its own nascent alcohol industry, America took 50 percent alcohol as the 100-proof point for spirits because at roughly 50 percent ABV a liquid can maintain combustion. So, 100 proof on the American scale represents 50 proof on the French scale and, to muddy the hydrometers even more, about 87.6 proof

on the British scale. America remains the only country in the world to use the proof system on its labels. The rest of the world adopted the French system of alcohol by volume, which the hydrometer scale measures.

On your next distillery tour, look for the hydrometer bobbing along in the try box or spirit safe, the collection container of raw spirit coming from the still. Also look for a grimace of confusion on the face of the tour guide when you mention Archimedes in a bathtub.

MIDDLE AGES

OLD JENEVER

THE MONKS OF THE MIDDLE AGES STILL EXERT TREMENDOUS INFLUence on our drinking habits. As we trace the journey of distillation, about six hundred years lie entirely in their hands. In it, the recreational drinking of spirits begins. One of the last stops before we arrive at modern whiskey brings us to Flanders, a region within Belgium and the Netherlands, and a spirit called jenever.

Jenever was a form of "the water of life": a distilled spirit imbued with flavorings from bark, herbs, berries, or roots. Organic oils needed to cover up the nasty, harsh, sulfury single pass through a crude alembic. With the development of high-proof, distilled alcohol as a solvent, we could leech those oils for curatives and ingest them in a more potent form. Juniper, from the bush of that name, was a favorite. Evidence of its use is found as far back as Mesopotamia

The Peasant Dance (1568) by Pieter Bruegel the Elder

and as wide as China to the Americas, Africa, and Europe. Its piney reviving scent helped make its leap through history. The evolution of modern medicine is replete with its use.

Jenever links us to whiskey because its earliest forms used malted grain as their base, specifically malt whiskey, called malt wine. In the modern taxonomy, old jenever uses 100 percent malted barley spirit. From the 1400s, in the Netherlands, old jenever ruled as the drink of choice. It helped make the leap from pure medicine to a good time. Glance at the raucous hedonism in any of Pieter Bruegel the Elder's peasant paintings and you can almost smell the jenever in the clay vessels that he depicted.

Over the centuries, jenever, sometimes "genever," morphed into gin, specifically the London-dry style. Jenever became a favorite of 19th-century drinkers and mixologists, including Jerry Thomas. He includes the spirit in more than a few recipes in his cocktail guide, the first ever published. But in the 1900s, confounded by Prohibition, jenever lost its way.

A new generation is discovering its pleasures, however. The latest incarnation comes from Philip Duff, a renowned bartender. His Old Duff Genever comes in two forms, old and new, and his old style uses 100 percent malt whisky as a base. It's an ancient crossover for the modern whiskey drinker.

CLOTH OF ARMAGNAC

DISTILLATION SEPARATES, CONCENTRATES, AND PURIFIES MINERALS or organic matter. Its beginnings lurk in the distant reaches of ancient Sumer, Egypt, and Persia. The peoples of those empires used heat, an open pot, and friction to "distill" sulfide minerals into antimony, a black powder that they applied around their eyes to ward off both desert and river blindness. Centuries later, that pot (the cucurbit) was combined with an alembic, an enclosure to trap condensation. In the 700s, Arabs carried the art and language of antimony with them on their conquests, through Asia Minor and into southern Europe. Their ownership of it gave us the word *alcohol,* from the Arabic *al kohl,* to blacken.

A new ingredient also entered the picture: wine. Distillers learned to isolate and concentrate its alcohol. A miraculous evolution of ancient faith and modern technology resulted. Antiseptic and pure, it cured, revived, and preserved. Transforming the four elements of the ancient world—earth, water, fire, and wind—into another form created this ethereal fifth element or quintessence, touched by the hand of their various gods. It became a spirit, a word that we still use today.

In the Middle Ages, the centers of distillation alchemy lay in southern Europe, where the legacy of Arabic learning and culture lingered. Abbeys and monasteries created institutions of learning that begat universities: Bologna, Salamanca, Padua, Naples, Valladolid, Coimbra. At their core stood the magical, transformative alembic. In the developing vocabulary of alchemy, the wolf had to drive impurities from the dragon to produce gold. Fueled by the alcohol in wine, alchemists harnessed thousands of years of herbalism to produce fire water, or *aygue ardente* in Medieval Latin.

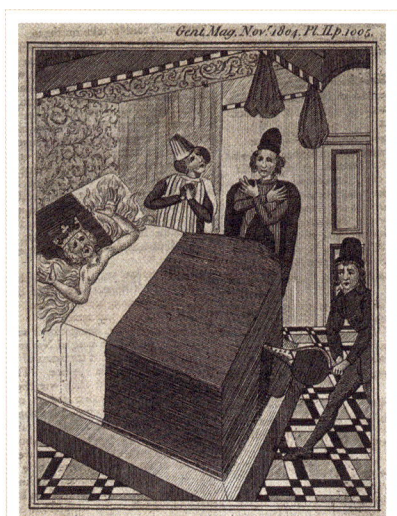

Experimentation was the order of the age, with mixed results. In 1387, in an attempt to drive the bad spirits from the

body of Charles II, aka Charles the Bad, ruler of Navarre, monl
wrapped his body in cloth soaked in aygue ardente and an herb
mixture. It accidentally caught fire, and he died an agonizing deat
The monks conceived of that cure from the writings of Vital du Fou
who in 1310, pronounced 40 different virtues using aygue ardente
According to the good doctor: "If one adds herbs, it extracts their
virtues and makes redness disappear and heat in the eyes. Frequent anointment of a paralyzed member will render it to its normal state." As long as no one is smoking nearby.

That aygue ardente now goes by the name Armagnac, the earthy, rich, aged brandy made in the Gascony region of France. Wine-based spirits precede grain-based ones by a few hundred years, so Armagnac serves as our link to aqua vitae and whiskey's beginnings. Dartigolongue, founded in 1838 and one of the oldest brandy houses in Bas-Armagnac, offers a perfect brandy crossover for the whiskey drinker looking to plumb the depths of history—from a safe distance of course.

Middle Ages

RENAISSANCE

LINDORES ABBEY

THERE'S NO STORY MORE REPEATED TO DEVOTEES OF SCOTCH WHISKY than the tale of its beginnings. Feel free to sing along:

> Eight bolls of malt
> for Friar John Cor
> to make aqua vitae
> in 1494.

The good friar was part of the Tironensian Order, established by St. Bernard of Abbeville in the early 1100s century in France. The order spread quickly to the British Isles and established numerous sites in Scotland, among them Lindores Abbey in Fife in 1191. In 1494, the Royal Exchequer, King James IV's accountant and taxman, opened his books to mark down the day's business: a payment made to Brother John Cor by receipt of the comptroller, as he asserts, "by order of the lord the king, to make aqua vitae within this account, eight bolls of malt." And that's how our good friar Jon Cor became a linchpin, with the first mention of whisky in Scottish history.

Less than a century later, the Protestant Reformation spelled doom for the abbey, which slowly declined, abandoned to history. In 1913, the great-grandfather of the current owner Andrew McKenzie Smith purchased the land along with the abbey ruins. The family farmed the land, and though they appreciated the beauty of the ruins they paid little attention to it or its history.

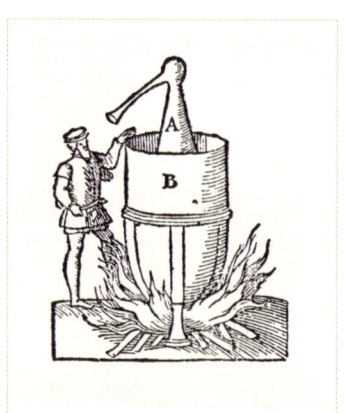

Then, one day in 2001, a man knocked on their front door and asked if he could stroll through the ruins. The man was the great whisky chronicler Michael Jackson. Less than a year later, he included his account of the story in his book, *Scotland and Its Whiskies*. That book opened the door through which we all have walked since then.

THE HISTORY OF WHISKEY

Lindores Abbey Distillery

McKenzie Smith made a few stabs at distillation before inviting another great name in the world of whisky to take part. Dr. Jim Swan, distillery consultant and the "Einstein of Whisky" (see page 196), arrived in 2013 to help establish what has become Lindores Abbey Distillery. In 2018, an archaeological dig into the land around the abbey unearthed a major discovery: a circle of rocks above the edge of a deep clay pot. A lab analysis of the pot found traces of carbon and barley, evidence of what everyone had expected. The long-lost distillery of Friar John Cor had come to light, and a legend had reverted to reality.

After a break of more than five hundred years, the single malts of Lindores Abbey are flowing again. Jackson died in 2007 and Swan in 2017, but McKenzie Smith, with the help of distillery manager Gary Haggart, has embraced the abbey's legacy and erected a beautiful new distillery on the property. The barley grows and is malted in the Fife region, and the well water comes from the same source used by the original abbey. They released their first bottling in 2021. The Roman numerals on the label, "MCDXCIV," refer to the exchequer's date, 1494. It's a sure bet that Swan, Jackson, and the good friar himself are watching over the operation and toasting with a dram raised to the new incarnation of Lindores Abbey.

BAROQUE ERA

SMUGGLERS' COMPANIONS

From the 1500s to the 1900s, smuggling was a way of life in the British Isles. Agents of the crown, seemingly everywhere, sought to create revenue for the royal coffers and to suppress competition from local artisans or foreign imports. They handed out licenses for any goods created or sold, whether wool or whiskey. They imposed import duties along coastlines where ships docked in established ports and harbors. Tax collectors, or gaugers, were everywhere. Robert Burns, the bard of Scotland, and Aeneas Coffey, who patented his famous still, both worked as gaugers.

For rural folk, distilling and smuggling went hand in hand. If distilling was seen as a birthright, passed from generation to generation, then smuggling was the literal rite of passage, enabling that noble tradition to continue. Smugglers needed creativity, guts, and an innate knowledge of local topography. They required bravery to handle the rigors of hijacking and thievery, and they needed specialized containers, called ankers and tubs, to store and transport their illicit cargo.

Legit dealers of goods used wooden barrels, large, heavy, and needing a team of men and winches to load them on and off ships or onto wagons. Barrels were obvious and therefore easy to manage, gauge, and tax. However, an anker contained only eight gallons, its sides purposely flattened to make it easy for one man to carry it. A tub contained half of that. Two men or one horse could carry four of them, roped together, allowing the smuggler to traverse the most difficult, remote terrain, out of the gauger's view.

An even more ingenious tool was the smuggler's barrel, with an internal structure that hid an important secret. A regular barrel is a simple vessel. It has three basic parts: long, flat staves of wood that have been curved by heat and fitted side by side into a circle; a series of ropes or metal bands around the staves to hold them together with pressure; and two heads on either end to seal the barrel. In the center of one stave, a drilled bunghole allows for filling and emptying it.

The smuggler's barrel converted that form into the ideal smuggler's companion. The interior contained two walls, made of wood, that separated it into three chambers. But those interior walls, rather than setting across the barrel, parallel to the heads, tilted outward from the inside of the bung out to the heads. The center portion, which was accessed by the bung, could contain water or even a low-tax wine. A gauge inserted to determine the contents would be tapped into the center portion. Any illicit contents in the outer compartments would go undiscovered, allowing a smuggler to continue merrily onward.

GRANDE CHARTREUSE

SINCE THE EARLY DAYS OF OUR SPECIES, WE LIVED WITH THE UNDERstanding that ingesting fermented beverages brought us to another sense of ourselves. Our guides on this journey were the holy men and women of our tribes. They administered the path toward this enlightenment, following the belief that it would bring us closer to whichever god we were seeking. In their hands, the cucurbit and the alembic, the forerunners of today's pot stills, were prime tools of the trade.

In 1054, Bruno de Cologne founded the Carthusian Order in the French Alps. Like many monastic orders, the brothers set their first duty to God, who commanded them with obedience. For the first five hundred years of their existence, they remained cloistered in a stretch of wilderness called the Désert de Chartreuse, where they farmed, raised cattle, and engaged in self-sufficiency crafts such as woodworking. Some monks contributed to the world a life of prayer, which they

undertook on behalf of the Church and the human race. Other brothers had less strict vows, doing the manual labor of food preparation, cooking, and cleaning. While still maintaining a vow of silence, they were slightly more connected to the outside world. Through this industrious, silent pathway, Chartreuse came to be, and with it, a link between distilled medicine and recreational drinking.

According to the story, François-Hannibal d'Estrées, marshal of King Henri IV's artillery, gave the order an ancient manuscript in 1605, called the "Elixir." It contained the recipe, using 130 herbs and methods preparing, macerating, and blending them into a tonic. The popularity of this crossover between medicine and beverage grew among locals. In 1764, the monks expanded their distilling facility and created green Chartreuse, as we know it today, which eventually spread worldwide.

   Green Chartreuse has served as a tonic, refresher, digestif, and cocktail ingredient for centuries. Along with Yellow—its less potent sibling, which debuted in 1840—it has survived revolutions, expulsions, and world wars, the secrets of its composition passed through the generations by a handful of Carthusian brothers. It made the leap from small craft to industrial manufacture with no change to the recipe, and is the perfect bottle to remind us of the role of the holy men and women who, through time, brought us our whiskey today.

CHARTER OF COLERAINE

IN THE FIRST DECADE OF THE 1600S, KING JAMES VI OF SCOTLAND (ALSO known as King James I of England and Ireland) had multiple goals for the northern region of Ireland: to suppress the native Gaels; to prove to the Scottish nobility that he hadn't forgotten them; and to "make better subjects" of the inhabitants of northern England and the Scottish Lowlands still mired in an Iron Age subsistence. One idea was to establish plantations on more than 1 million acres in the province of Ulster, cede the land to governors loyal to the crown to oversee it, import subjects needing a better life, and breed the natives out of existence. Loyalists received royal charters to do as they pleased as long as tax revenue made its way back to royal coffers. Those privileges included a royal warrant to establish a distillery. In 1608, Thomas Phillips, one of the governors, received one such

charter in the "country of Coleraine," but he led such an unsettled life that he traded it for another parcel. If he produced any whiskey there, it's lost to time.

But the charter stayed in place as new governors came to Ulster to oversee a stew of religious and cultural upheaval (after King Henry VIII of England and Ireland broke with Rome in 1534, the Catholic and Anglican faiths had been jostling for power). The new generations of the north learned to farm, and from displaced clerics they learned to make "mountain dew" from malted barley wines. Oppressive taxes led them to develop a different style, called *poitín*, made from other grains, as well. They also adopted the Presbyterianism born in the kirks (churches) of the Scottish Lowlands. A century later, subsequent generations established their own culture: brittle and warlike, itinerant and self-sufficient, fiercely loyal

THE HISTORY OF WHISKEY

to leadership and abhorrent of outside rule. These Scots-Irish, one of the largest immigrant populations to the Western Hemisphere, crossed the Atlantic, and they knew how to make whiskey.

Back in the northern part of Ireland, with the troublemakers out of the way, the distilling warrant of that royal charter of Coleraine finally went into effect in 1748. It allowed for the creation of Bushmills, close by Giant's Causeway and blessed with the resilience to withstand neglect, catastrophic fires, American Prohibition, World War II bombings, takeovers by Seagram, Irish Distillers, Pernod Ricard, and Diageo. In the early days, as loyalists, they paid every malt tax and stayed true to the original *uisce beatha* of their ancestors, producing only triple-distilled malt whiskey. If only Sir Thomas proved as hardy as they had.

Baroque Era

OUR ANCESTORS HOLLOWED GOURDS THEN USED TOOLS TO FASHION vessels from wood or stone to hold liquids. Eventually we learned to manufacture cups using clay, gold, copper, bronze, iron, and glass. Integrated into community rituals, these cups took on vast significance. In some cases, they rose to the highest realms of conscious activities, a way to communicate with unseen forces or commemorate events of importance: the act of bringing a liquid to our lips. They proved as integral to civilization as they had been to our survival.

No one knows for certain exactly how the quaich, one of those vessels, came about, but it's Celtic Gaelic in origin. A shallow bowl originally carved from wood, it has flat panels coming from two sides of the lip with which to hold it. Its name derives from *cuach*, the Gaelic word for "cup." Researchers think that the form derived from seashells, which would put its origins with the ancient Celtic tribes, indigenous Picts, or the Scoti who inhabited the northern coasts of the British Isles. It may have evolved from vessels used by Druid priests or Viking raiders. Again, no one knows for certain, but its importance has inspired a modern group of Scotch whisky enthusiasts to name their association after it: the Keepers of the Quaich. It functioned as a toasting vessel, and it was used in ceremony, feasting, and welcoming. Historians believe that clan chieftains used it as a signifier of rank and clan importance, which leads us to an anecdote referencing one of its many purported uses.

In Scotland, Highland clans constantly fought one another. Battles, wars, and other acts of violence formed a regular part of life. At some point, the acrimony came to an end, but suspicions and ulterior motives always provided fodder for new conflict. Clan leaders had the responsibility of ending hostilities and keeping a lasting peace. On a field of battle, two warring tribes faced each other, and from the ranks, the clan chieftains emerged, each holding his quaich high, filled to the brim with whisky, mead, or beer. They marched to the center and, face to face, shared an oath for peace. They banged their quaiches together, each spilling his liquid into the other's vessel, and drank. This act signaled to the troops that there would be no poisoning one another at the banquet that evening. Trust held fast, and peace endured. *Slàinte!*

Baroque Era

THE FIRST FAMILIES OF WHISKY

IN 1066, WILLIAM, DUKE OF NORMANDY AND A DESCENDANT OF VIKING conquerors, mounted an invasion that charted the course of whiskey (and history) in the British Isles. In the company of William came a knight called Petrus de Haga, whose anglicized name became Haig. The Haigs moved into the Lowland Scottish Borders, establishing themselves there for generations as lairds of Bemersyde. One of their number fought alongside William Wallace at the Battle of Stirling Bridge.

In the 1600s, Robert Haig got into a tussle at home, left for the Netherlands, where he learned to distill, and returned to Alloa in the Lowlands. He ran afoul of the Scottish kirk—because he was Catholic and they weren't—for distilling on the Sabbath: "his cauldron on fyre and a stand reiking." This indictment is the first time that the act of distilling appears in print. The Haigs continued distilling at a farm-craft level for generations until the mid-1800s.

The Steins, another Lowland farmer family, trace their roots to the Danish coast. After the Reformation, they took over the old monastery in Kennetpans on the River Forth, about halfway between Edinburgh and Glasgow. According to lore, the good friars there taught the Steins the art of distillation before they abandoned the site. By the 1730s, Andrew Stein had created the largest commercial distillery in Scotland, second only to Kilbagie, down the river, which he also owned. In Kennetpans, distilling grew from a farm craft to a commercial industry. John Stein, Andrew's grandson, later skipped across the North Channel and established the Bow Street Distillery in Dublin.

As the first families of whisky, the Haigs and Steins have influenced it in every Western country that makes it. It took generations, but here's how it all came together. John Haig, Robert's great-great-grandson, married Margaret Stein in 1751. The couple had 10 children by the time John died, and their Stein uncles took all five sons under their wing, training them as distillers at Kennetpans and Kilbagie.

In the 1820s, Robert Stein, owner of Kilbagie, came across a diagram of a continuous operating still patented by Jean-Baptiste Cellier-Blumenthal. Cellier-Blumenthal's invention, a single-pass column still separated by copper plates, separated beet sugar from beets and purified it. Stein modified the design for grain mash and patented it for whisky in 1826. His cousin John Haig installed it in his new distillery, Cameronbridge, but it wasn't a smashing success. The single pass couldn't clean the sulfur from the grain mash. A few years later, Aeneas Coffey, an Irish tax collector, doubled Stein's single column, and voilà. The Coffey still eventually became the modern column still, today's workhorse for Scotch, Irish whiskey, Kentucky bourbon, Canadian whisky, and more.

Find yourself a dram of Cameron Brig, a rare single-grain Scotch from Cameronbridge, while you mull the secret to founding a whiskey dynasty: Marry the right person.

A POT OF POITÍN

ALL EVIDENCE POINTS TO *UISCE BEATHA*—THE GAELIC "WATER OF LIFE," which we call whiskey—bubbling from Ireland first. Rurally it was called poitín (PAH-cheen), which means "pot" in Gaelic. The pots consisted of copper or tin, and the spirit came from whatever grains, roots, or fruits that were available.

Poitín was formulated by the monastic clergymen of the Roman Church, cast out from their cloistered cells after King Henry VIII disbanded the religious orders in 1534. Dublin especially was a stronghold for the Church in its creation of the "Liberties." The Liberties were medieval land parcels set on the outskirts of the city and overseen by a "lord" who was designated by the Church to create its own economy and enterprise zone. Its cathedrals and abbeys were centerpieces of knowledge, faith, and commerce. As a port city, Dublin was at the crossroads of a thriving economy, and as such, their "Liberties" attracted artisans, activists, and a bolder way of living. Within the walls of the abbeys, the monks practiced the arts of brewing, beekeeping, and animal husbandry. They compounded herbs into ancient pharmaceutical remedies, integrating their understanding of distillation to extract purer elixirs. After their expulsion, they spread out into the countryside, itinerant handymen with centuries of mystical knowledge, eager to make a living.

This is how distillation spread to the everyday farmer, turning their crude ales and wines from their crops into poitín. It was medicine evolving to recreation, and the "burn" you received from drinking it was proof that it was rooting out the evil spirits inside of you. That sensation came from drinking the "heads," filled with methanol, the first cut of liquid from a single pass through the pot. The idea of the Irish "wakes" arose from this, as many people were temporarily poisoned from drinking the heads, putting their "dead drunk" bodies into a type of suspension. Gravediggers had found scratches on the insides of coffins from people who awoke after being buried alive. So a little bell would be placed in their

coffin, should they wake up, making them a "dead ringer" who could be "saved by the bell." After some time, the farmers learned that the best poitín came after the heads, in the second cut, causing them to "throw one out for the bhoys," casting the heads out to the whiskey fairies with the result being "smoother." In 1661, after the restoration of King Charles II to the thrones of England, Scotland, and Ireland, Irish Parliament levied a hefty tax on poitín that effectively banned it.

Poitín didn't evolve into Ireland's great pot-still whiskey in the same way that malt whisky did in the glens and hollows of the Scottish Highlands. For Ireland to lead the whiskey world in the 1800s, poitín had to

Simple farm distillation equipment like this produced poitín.

return to its roots in Dublin, setting a course for the Big Four of whiskey dominance: Jameson (John and William), Powers, and Roe. More about them later. Today, in Dublin's Bar 1661, owner Dave Mulligan is reviving the poitín tradition with Bán 1661, named for the date of the infamous excise tax and offering a new take on craft cocktails. The monks of Dublin would approve.

THE TAXMAN COMETH

IN THE WESTERN WORLD, THREE PEOPLE DEVELOPED WHISKEY. THE farmer grew grain and fermented excess into beer. The distiller purified that beer into a stronger, more stable, more versatile spirit that became more valuable than the grain that made it. The tax collector pursued revenue from those distilled spirits, which forced the distiller to innovate or change to stay within the bounds of the tax code or to avoid detection. If a crown or government passed a law to protect or define whiskey, its original purpose for doing so was to collect the tax on it and fill the coffers.

From the beginning, Irish distillers had been experimenting with multiple grains in their mash bills. However, in 1697, a malt tax levied on English brewers prompted the Irish to normalize the use of unmalted or "green" barley in their poitín. In 1785, another malt tax legitimized commercial distillation, but a century of dodging the taxable ingredient had acclimated Irish palates to the unmalted style, which blends a spicy, oily grassiness with the fruity creaminess of the smaller malted portion. That style crowned Dublin and Cork as the whiskey centers of the world in the mid-1800s.

In Scotland, whisky taxes led to a litany of irony. Every tax that the Scottish or British government imposed to control or end unlicensed stills or smuggled whisky inadvertently made the smuggled stuff better. The 1713 malt tax spurred riots in Edinburgh and Glasgow and *increased* the number of illicit Highland stills. Taxes on

Tax collectors' coffers overflowed during distillation season.

still size, capacity, and even location led to the creation of a "noxious" spirit in the Lowlands (mostly headed to England for rectification into gin) that used very little malt, and a more flavorful one in the Highlands that used mostly malt.

The governments of Britain and Ireland unified in 1800, and in 1823 Parliament passed An Act to Grant Certain Duties of Excise upon Spirits Distilled from Corn or Grain in Scotland and Ireland. That legislation set a licensing fee for stills, duty levels for distilled grain spirits, and allowed for warehousing spirits before payment. This act finally brought the lawlessness under control and literally brought the Scotch whisky industry into being.

In 1878, Canada became the first country to guarantee the quality of their whisky with their own excise tax, which required a minimum of two years of aging (extended to three in 1890). In America, the Bottled in Bond Act, passed in 1897, guaranteed a minimum of four years of aging and other details that safeguarded quality and flavor.

Across the Western world, the 20th century brought new meaning to the word *pure*. Beginning in 1901, Britain and Canada established new definitions for the term. In America, the Pure Food and Drug Act of 1906 ratified whiskey's legal definition as a grain-based distillate, and in 1936, the creation of the Federal Alcohol Administration brought further clarification to bourbon, rye, wheat, and straight whiskey that we still follow today. You can curse Tax Day if you choose but pour some out for the tax collector because he's why your favorite whiskey tastes so good.

RUMBULLION TO RYE

THE RISE OF WHISKEY IN THE WESTERN HEMISPHERE OWES A DEBT to the rum trade. Seafaring European kingdoms—Portugal, Spain, the Netherlands, France, and England/Britain—fought over the lands of the New World. When you follow the money, it all comes down to the intertwined trade of sugar, a luxury commodity, and the people enslaved to produce and harvest it.

Transported from West Africa to the tropical regions of the Americas, slaves harvested sugarcane, which merchants shipped to ports along the Atlantic Coast, from Savannah to Nova Scotia, for processing. From there, sugar, the finished product, was shipped around the world. Refining sugar creates molasses as a by-product, and distilling molasses creates rumbullion, known today as rum. The English loved rum. They ejected the Dutch from New Amsterdam in 1664, and that year a rum still started production on Staten Island. The English and, after 1707, British Navy mandated a "daily tot" of rum for every sailor, a tradition that lasted into the 1970s.

In the American colonies, where molasses flowed easily, the landed gentry toasted with rum-based liquors, punches, and other drinks. Rum soon became a key industry and trading commodity of British North America—but with obstacles. In 1733, the British passed the Molasses Act, which taxed the importation of any non-British sugar, molasses, or rum into the colonies in order to preserve their monopoly. This act created a black market that smuggled those commodities from Dutch and French colonies in the Caribbean, which the British government addressed with an amended Sugar Act in 1764. Same tax, different name.

In the early 1700s, two immigrant groups began their sojourn to the New World: the Scots-Irish and various groups of Germans. Outcasts in New England, both groups brought their distilling traditions and their versions of "mountain dew" and *kornschnappes* with them. Neither group had a taste for rum. As they pressed west, over Pennsylvania's Allegheny Mountains, farther from coastal ports, molasses became more difficult and

A sugar mill on the island of Guadeloupe in the Caribbean.

expensive to transport. As they separated physically from the British-influenced East Coast, their ideological independence grew. They turned to readily available crops, choosing rye: regionally accessible, cheap, and definitely not rum. That change in tastes lasted for 150 years.

For more than 30 years, Ed Hamilton, the "minister of rum," has been traveling in the Caribbean and curating rums. His West Indies 1670 Blend combines high-proof Guyanese and aged Jamaican rums in a union of cultural styles. The date in the name commemorates the founding of the distilleries that make the source rums, which have witnessed much of rum history, including the rebellion against it that sparked the northern love of rye.

RYES OF THE MENNONITES

IN THE WESTERN WORLD, THE HISTORY OF WHISKEY ENTWINES TIGHTLY with religion—not with faith but with the orders that maintained the faith. In the 700s, the followers of Muhammad carried distillation from the Arabian Peninsula to the lands of their conquests. The holy men of the fading Byzantine Empire absorbed their gifts and transmitted them to the monks and priests of the emerging Holy Roman Empire. For the next five hundred years, as they translated the esoterica of Arabic writings, these holy men deepened their understanding of aqua vitae. That knowledge spread through Europe and the British Isles and to the far reaches of the Church's evangelism.

The Protestant Reformation completely realigned religious and philosophical thinking in Europe, however. From cloistered quarters, the secrets of distillation ventured into the realms of common people. Aqua vitae became uisce beatha (in Gaelic) and continued its medicinal path, but a new form of the drink emerged: whiskey, a drink for pleasure. For many Protestants, it encouraged the baser instincts of man, giving them good reason to suppress its use. But for others, making and drinking it converged with their understanding of individual choice as the foundation of their faith. Of the many Protestant sects, Anabaptism followed this line of thought, and from the Anabaptists came the Mennonites, who laid the foundations of rye whiskey in Pennsylvania.

In 1681, William Penn founded Pennsylvania on a principle of religious freedom, setting the stage for a century of migrations from the Scots-Irish and both Catholic and Protestant Germans. From northern Germanic lands, the legacy of the Mennonites still reverberates today. The Schenks, Bombergers, and Overholts, all distilling families, escaped religious oppression in Europe. In America, they collectively became responsible for the iconic, all-rye mash bill that brought commercial success to Pennsylvania rye whiskey, which lasted until Prohibition. After Repeal in 1933, the Overholts faded, and the Shenck/Bomberger distillery transformed first into Pennco and then the original Michter's Distillery before that closed in 1989.

Revived in the 1990s in Kentucky, the new Michter's has released Shenk's Homestead as part of their legacy series, in homage to John Shenk, who founded

the original distillery in Schaefferstown, Pennsylvania, in 1753. Made primarily of corn, with some malted rye, and prepared with the sour-mash method, it fits Kentucky's climate better than Pennsylvania's, but we still can raise it to toast the spirit of Mennonite ingenuity and faith.

INDUSTRIAL AGE

WORM TUB

DISTILLATION PURIFIES BY SEPARATING AND REUNITING: HEAT SOMEthing high enough that the molecules disassemble and come back together as something else. With whiskey, disassembly separates ethanol gas from the water that makes up the beer in the still while retaining the heavier flavor molecules of the grain that makes whiskey. The process needs the proper environment to turn the gas into liquid again.

In the history of distillation, that journey took maybe a thousand years. If a pot boiled over a fire, the steam dissipated into the air. To hold the escaping element, we capped that pot with the alembic, then attached a pipe to the top in which the steam collected and naturally cooled into drops of liquid (*stilla* in Latin). In the early Middle Ages, the device was called a lute, then a retort, and Latin described that action as *distillare,* "to drip from." In cooler air, the pipe produced a flow rather than just droplets. Applying wet sponges and rags cooled the pipe, but the improvements didn't produce enough yield to warrant the effort and time. If the air isn't cool all the time, how do you create that same condition when desired?

The answer to that simple question brings us to the "worm," a snaking helix of copper that distillers attached to their stills. In the Middle Ages, Italian chemists recognized what it did: condensing gas back to liquid form using metal and glass formations.

The worm tub was the preferred method of cooling down distillate from the early 1800s, and as distillers became more sophisticated with copper, they coiled the pipe and set it in a tub of cool water. Now, using a worm tub, they could dismantle the still quickly, throw everything in the back of the wagon, and flee before revenue agents spotted them. That sufficed until the arrival of the shell and tube condenser in the 1900s. The series of identical copper tubes in a cold

water "shell" was much more efficient in cleaning out the "bad notes" of the distillate than a single coil. But some distilleries have held onto their worms, notably Knockdhu, Talisker, and Springbank in Scotland.

This whisky is Craigellachie 13 year, a single malt from Scotland. It is one of the "fingerprint" malts that makes up Dewar's Blended Scotch. They still use an old iron worm in their worm tub. The iron holds on to funkier flavors and transforms them into other phenolics that give it its heavy, "meaty" taste.

CUMBERLAND GAP

I**N 1700s VIRGINIA, CORN MEANT SURVIVAL. YOU COULD GRIND THE** kernels and mill them into flour to make bread or soak them in lye or wood ash and cook them into hominy. The stalks fed livestock. The shucks filled

mattresses or—when dried, lashed together, and tarred—created thatched roofing. Anything left over, the "middlings," became whiskey.

The mythologies around the "first" distiller miss the point. People distilled to live. Distilling meant bartering, and whiskey functioned as currency: one more survival skill giving you one more day on a dangerous frontier. The lucky, thrifty, crafty, or all three hauled stills with them as they migrated westward over the Appalachian Mountains. A still was as valuable as a horse for survival.

Born around 1760, Wattie Boone often receives credit as the first person to produce bourbon. Researchers have sketched him only around the edges because we have so little to fill in the blanks with certainty. He may have been related to Daniel

Boone. Thomas Lincoln, father of the president, may have worked for him. Many historians place his distillery at the point where Knob Creek and Pottinger's Mill Road meet in Kentucky, a point now lost in time. Wattie Boone the man was real, though, and made his way with others through the Cumberland Gap to the advancing frontier. Corn gave them all the means to survive another day, and he made whiskey, not bourbon. We can be sure of this simply because bourbon doesn't appear in writing until 1821.

Where, then, do we get the idea of a Wattie Boone? In the 1950s and '60s, bourbon brands were flexing marketing muscles that had atrophied during Prohibition and World War II. The new consumer economy was growing and, as today, tidbits of the people who made history gave a familiar warmth to something new or scarce. They created the whiskey "backstory," teeming with firsts: first distiller, first distillery, first charred barrel, and so on. Many of those midcentury companies produce today's favorite brands. All of them missed the mark by a few degrees, but when it comes to marketing, you only need to get close to the mark to win.

In 1992, Jim Beam introduced a bourbon called Knob Creek, nodding to a vestige of Boone's existence. Now part of Suntory Global Spirits, the company makes no mention of Wattie in their marketing materials, but that wasn't the idea. Knob Creek is a real place. At one time, someone made whiskey there, and for marketing purposes, that's enough.

BOW STREET DISTILLERY

IT PAYS TO MARRY WELL. THE FIRST INTERMARRIAGE AMONG THE FIRST families of whiskey occurred in 1751 when John Haig, great-great grandson of Robert Haig, married Margaret Stein, who bore 10 children. Their eldest daughter, also Margaret, met John Jameson, sheriff of Clackmannan, a small town near Stirling in the Scottish Lowlands. That prominent position allowed him to cavort with the best of society, rubbing elbows with the elite. John Jameson and young Margaret Haig married in 1768, and they had 16 children.

In the 1760s, taxes raised their hydra head again in a series of excise acts that pressured Lowland distillers, squeezing profits and bankrupting a few of them. The Stein and Haig dynasties were operating in their fourth and fifth generations when the Steins cast the family eye across the North Channel to Ireland. In 1780, they opened the Bow Street Distillery in Dublin, the island's biggest city. Seeing an opportunity, John Jameson and family moved there and became manager of the distillery in 1788. By 1805, he took full ownership and, in 1810, renamed the enterprise John Jameson and Son. (Note the parallels between his story and Joseph Seagram.) Under Jameson's leadership, the Bow Street Distillery became the linchpin of Dublin's Golden Triangle boom that dominated the whiskey world in the 1800s. A six-acre site, Bow Street had one of Ireland's largest cattle markets sitting on its doorstep. It also had a straight shot to the River Liffey and the Irish Sea.

But at that time, Dublin contained some of the worst slums in the Western world. Altruism compelled Jameson, an upright churchman, to take care of those who took care of him. He created a company town for his workers—but not an exploitative "company store" model. He built housing for them and their families. As they aged, workers progressively filled softer jobs so they could continue to make a living. At any given time, more than three hundred men were working at the distillery, the second largest in the Triangle after John Power's on John's Lane.

When John Jameson II took over at Bow Street, he fully adopted the rich mixture of malted and unmalted barley, the pot-still style that became standard for the Big Four of Dublin (John and William Jameson, Power, and Roe). They shipped their whiskey via cask, not bottle, so they needed to maintain quality in the pubs

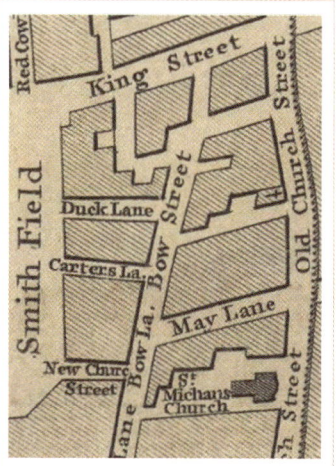

and inns that dispensed it. They sent out teams of "pub spies," who gathered samples, returned to the distillery lab, and tested them. We'll look at changes in the Dublin style next, but Jameson's newly released Single Pot Still Whiskey honors their founder, who married well and made the best of it.

THE GOLDEN TRIANGLE

IN 1534, KING HENRY VIII OF ENGLAND AND IRELAND DISSOLVED THE authority of the Catholic Church in his realms, closing the abbeys and monasteries. The monks took their knowledge of uisce beatha, the water of life, into the countryside, across the water to the Scottish Isles, into Wales, and to England. The Dublin Liberties, the enterprise districts once blessed by both King and the Church transferred to the private ownership of various lords. Their descendants developed the city, and three centuries later, Dublin was thriving again. To thrive is to drink. First came beer, then, under the patronage of a new set of brewers and distillers, whiskey.

In 1757, Peter Roe bought a small distillery with a massive smock windmill that, a century later, became the largest distillery in the world. In 1759, Arthur Guinness secured a 9,000-year lease on a brewery in St. James Gate. (Some 150 years later, his descendants bought out Roe, his neighbor, with whom he'd quarreled for years.) Next to arrive, in 1780, came John Jameson from Scotland to run his family's Bow Street Distillery. By the mid-1800s, his sons had turned that enterprise into the second-largest distillery and most popular whiskey in Ireland. When Walter Teeling arrived in 1782, an area called the Golden Triangle—extending from the Liberties, across the River Liffey, to Newmarket—contained some 37 distilleries. On John's Lane, James Power opened what became the Powers Distillery in 1791, the last of the bunch only because he'd been operating a tavern selling other people's whiskey for years.

Dublin's dominance in whiskey lasted for more than one hundred years. It took the ancient, rough poitín of the countryside and transformed it into the pot-still style that won the world's palate, from Tsar Peter the Great of Russia to whiskey expert and author Alfred Barnard. The distilleries of the Golden Triangle employed massive pot stills to circumvent excise taxes and adopted triple distillation to calm the roughness of the spirit. Irish whiskey became synonymous with quality, so much so that, when the phylloxera plague hit the vineyards of France in the 1860s, Irish whiskey replaced French brandy at the tables of the nobles and bourgeoisie of the Second Empire. Irish whiskey made its way into America with such a force that some American whiskeys called themselves "Irish." At home, Irish distillers treated their workers nobly, and examples abound of the altruism that they exhibited toward them.

As we'll see, the 1900s brought a host of troubles that led to the near extinction of Irish whiskey, but Ireland in the 21st century now boasts more than 45 distilleries. Through the haze of history, a taste of today's Powers John's Lane Single Pot Still Irish Whiskey serves as the best reminder of how Dublin once ruled the whiskey world with Liberties and whiskey for all.

THE HARBORMASTER

IN THE EARLIEST DAYS OF AMERICAN COMMERCE, ROUTES TO MARKET usually followed waterways. In postcolonial America, the Ohio River created mythologies. In it, fact and legend intertwined to become reality. From its origin in Pittsburgh, the Ohio meanders north then courses south and west. It provides a natural boundary for several states before rushing to the Mississippi River. This river pathway remains relatively unobstructed, allowing for flatboats filled with goods for sale to travel between Pittsburgh and the port of New Orleans—excepting for a two-and-a-half-mile stretch of pure limestone terror and destruction called the Falls of Ohio. It's a place that gave rise to Louisville and a Welsh immigrant named Evan Williams.

Rushing over a ridge of limestone, the falls stretch across the Ohio River from shore to shore and around the bend that makes up Louisville's northern end. When the water level ran low, most of the rocks were visible, presenting three channels or chutes to navigate. To do so, ships emptied their cargo on the shore, which was portaged downriver while the flatboats floated empty through the chutes. It offered an ideal opportunity for business, particularly carting, transportation, and hospitality. A choke point, the Falls of Ohio effectively controlled all commerce on one of America's most important waterways. To regulate and maintain safety, a harbormaster oversaw the operation. In 1797, that man was Evan Williams.

Today, people make much of Williams as the inspiration for his eponymous bourbon, but we know little about his distilling efforts, their effect and impact lost to time. But for a distiller in charge of the growing nation's most important westward port, it's not difficult to see the future: Whiskey Row. The port of Louisville became an obvious trade town for distillers and merchants all along the Ohio and points east. Wherever cargo and people come ashore, an economy pops up to support them and their safety. In this case, the

Diorama showing the Falls of the Ohio in the days of Evan Williams, with Louisville at the lower left. A set of locks and canals has since tamed the river.

harbormaster became not just the agent of growth in a frontier town but probably its law and justice, as well. Williams had power.

In 1957, when the folks at Heaven Hill Distillery read through the annals of history to find someone for whom to name their new whiskey, they came upon an obscure note about Williams and his first "commercial" distilling license, granted in 1783. From there, the mythology grew, as did the popularity of Heaven Hill's Evan Williams Bourbon, an international favorite. But they missed the real story: Evan Williams, a powerful harbormaster, enabled the growth of Louisville and Whiskey Row—except that story won't sell whiskey.

ALL THE PRESIDENT'S WHISKEY

A COUNTRY GENTLEMAN TRAINED AS A SURVEYOR, GEORGE WASH-ington also served in the Virginia Regiment. A loyal British subject, he, like other farmers, first grew tobacco, switching to wheat in 1765 when the markets changed. As a young major in the British Army during the French and Indian War he fought on the front lines of the conflict in the Ohio Valley and Western Pennsylvania. In that region, a confluence of Germans, Czechs, Scots-Irish, and Swiss immigrants farmed the land and made whiskey, mostly from rye, which grew abundantly there.

One of the first acts of his presidency directly affected them. Spurred by Secretary of the Treasury Alexander Hamilton to pay down the debt from the War of Independence, Congress instituted the nation's first excise tax on its own whiskey. Washington then had to put down the rebellion in Western Pennsylvania that came from that legislation.

After two terms as president, Washington returned to his farm in Mt. Vernon, which was barely profitable. It had a grain mill with two grinding stones, an automated grain elevator, a 16-foot water wheel, and could produce 3,200 pounds of meal per day—but it needed something else. Washington hired James Anderson to run the farm and bring it to profitability, and he immediately suggested building a distillery. Anderson oversaw the installation of two pot stills, and in 1798, the first president of the United States of America was making 4,500 gallons of rye whiskey. The next year, three more stills increased that yield to 10,942 gallons, and, yes, he paid the tax on it. His main customer was George Gilpin, a merchant in nearby Alexandria.

Washington died in December 1799 at age 67. The distillery maintained operations until fire destroyed it and the grain mill in 1814, marking an end to an ironic, obscure chapter of American history. But the 20th century reawakened an interest in its story. Using archaeological and documentary evidence, the grist mill was restored in 1932. A dig on the old distillery lasted nine years, uncovering the original stone foundation and evidence of five stills and boilers. In 2007, the distillery was reconstructed completely, built to the same specifications that Anderson himself had laid out.

Steve Bashore, a local miller with experience in restored machinery, ran the operation. Starting in 2009, he invited distillers from around the world to take part in making whiskey there: Dave Pickerell from Maker's Mark, Jimmy Russell from Wild Turkey, Lisa Roper from Widow Jane, and Bill Lumsden from Glenmorangie. That first year, they filled 200 barrels, and you can buy their first distillations at the distillery and in the wider Virginia area. The folks in Western Pennsylvania wish them well—no hard feelings over whiskey.

OLD OVERHOLTS

RYE WHISKEY WAS BECOMING THE PREFERRED DISTILLED SPIRIT OF the Western Pennsylvania frontier. Thomas Jefferson's administration repealed the excise tax and, as a result, legal distilling in the first decade of the new century moved from farm craft to cottage industry. From Bucks County, on the eastern side of the state, Henrich Oberholzer, a Mennonite, and his family moved into this region. They anglicized their name to Overholt and began distilling soon after settling. Within a short time, Henrich's son Abraham increased capacity and paid to haul a few barrels of finished whiskey over the Allegheny Mountains to the gentlemen's clubs of Philadelphia and Baltimore. Western-style rye whiskey was gaining popularity, and production in America was about to soar. Under Abraham, the Overholts became America's first commercial distilling success.

The common mash bill of that era consisted of 80 percent rye grain with 20 percent rye malt or barley malt—no corn. In 1859, the distillery moved from its origins in West Overton to nearby Broad Ford and installed cutting-edge technology: a three-chamber still that significantly increased volume. It sat on the Youghiogheny River, a tributary of the Monongahela River that flowed north to the Ohio River in Pittsburgh. This location afforded the Overholts the opportunity to ship their whiskey down the Ohio to New Orleans and beyond.

Imitators and competitors soon took notice, creating the regional designation of Monongahela rye or Pennsylvania rye. By 1894, dozens of distilleries were making and bottling rye whiskey on the river or nearby. Finch, Dillinger, Large, Grey, Vandergrift, Schenley, Gibson, Guckenheimer, Thompson, and more turned small family operations into commercial entities. In Scotland, the River Spey was the locus of Highland malt making that advanced whisky there. In the US, the Monongahela did that for rye. After World War II, the Broad Ford distillery closed, and the brand changed hands a few times until Beam picked it up and moved distilling operations to Kentucky. By the 1980s, the rye in Old

THE HISTORY OF WHISKEY

Overholt had reduced to its legal minimum of 51 percent, and corn and malted barley had replaced the rye malt. America had lost its collective taste for rye. The few bottlings available during the latter half of the 1900s were reduced with neutral spirits and sold as blends.

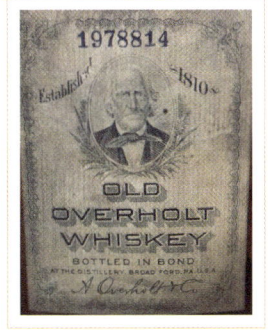

The craft cocktail renaissance brought rye back to prominence, however. In the early 2000s, Old Overholt appeared in good cocktails in line with their original, pre-Prohibition recipes. The discovery of barrels of high-quality rye aging at the old Seagram distillery in Indiana led to new rye brands forming: Redemption, James E. Pepper 1776, High West, and many others. In 2024, new owner Suntory reformulated A. Overholt to its original mash bill of 80 percent rye and 20 percent malt, revived as Monongahela Mash. Rumor has it that, on the label, Abraham's stern visage perked up a little at the news.

WALKER'S GROCER'S SHOP

EVERY MAJOR WHISKEY NATION HAS RULING FAMILIES. AMERICA HAS the Beam-Noe family; Canada has the Bronfmans; Ireland's trinity consists of the Jamesons, Powers, and Roes. In Japan, the Torii family has overseen Suntory for four generations. In Scotland, the Haigs, Steins, and Dewars kept their influence alive for two hundred years. But one brand truly conquered the world with its family name: the Walkers.

Most great brand stories have humble beginnings. The Walker family owned a dairy farm, and when Alexander Walker died in 1819, his young son John left to find his fortune. With family backing, he bought an Italian grocer's shop in Kilmarnock, Scotland, giving us a crossover connection to the 19th-century merchant store (another set of dynasties). Distillers made the whiskey, but grocers created the whiskey industry. As John Walker bought, sold, and traded teas, spices, and other merchandise from around the world, he taught himself to blend the rough, hard-edged smoke bombs of the Highlands into consumer-friendly whiskies. After the Coffey still made lighter grain whiskies from the Lowlands more available, Walker's business moved away from food and closer to defining what we drink as whisky today.

For that, we look to his son Alexander, who transformed his father's storefront into a worldwide brand. Trained as a blender by his father and later apprenticing with an independent broker, the young Walker created some of the key assets that we still admire today. In the 1860s, he innovated the square bottle and the 24-degree angle on the label to distinguish his first commercial blend, Old Highland Whisky, from others sold in bottles instead of casks. Export sales were becoming big business, and Walker secured transport of his barrels as ballast for schooners, received by his shipping agent on the other end. Created by illustrator Tom Browne, the Striding Man on the label came in 1908, and Johnnie Walker appeared in 1909.

The bane of a brand is inconsistency, and a blender must ensure that every batch meets the company standard. To

Four generations of the Walker family—John (1805–1857), Alexander (1837–1889), George (1864–1926), Alexander II (1869–1950)—presiding over a line-up of Johnnie Walker whiskies.

safeguard consistency and to stave off price fluctuations, the company purchased a series of distilleries: first Cardhu, the heart of the blend; then Clynelish, Talisker, and others that still make up the "fingerprints" of Johnnie Walker's core line of Red, Black, and Blue labels. Alexander Walker brought his three sons into the business, which continued its domination until its absorption in 1925 into the powerful Distillers Company Ltd. (DCL), now Diageo. The sons also rise, and Johnnie keeps walking. In their inventory today, Johnnie Walker has more than 10 million casks managed by master blender Emma Walker, no relation. Four generations of Walkers, a brand spanning three centuries, and more than three hundred bottles sold in the time that it took you to read this essay. That's some serious striding.

SPIRIT SAFE

FEW WORDS IN THE ENGLISH LANGUAGE GENERATE MORE HATE THAN the word *tax*. But taxes, an unwanted catalyst of evolution, advanced whiskey in Scotland and Ireland. The 1785 malt tax imposed in Ireland pushed more farmers to adopt unmalted barley in their mash as a revolt, creating the pot-still style that propelled Irish whiskey to world-class status. In Scotland, the Wash Act of 1784 formally delineated the Highlands from the Lowlands. The crown assessed Highlanders on the amount of malt and size of the still rather than on its output. Each new rule forced them to innovate to duck the excise, cooking up new ways to make their "mountain dew from only malted barley." The result: their malt was favored more than Lowland whiskies that used any fodder of grains and treacle to make it more cheaply, and therefore, more tax compliant.

Methods to calculate the tax looked like a scattershot ramble of whatever technology was available and the skill (and honesty) of the assessor. Then a series of patents sprang up that promised to address both issues. In 1819, James Fox applied for a patent in Scotland for a type of sealed lockbox attached to the end of the worm tub. The resulting liquid went into three different cisterns: one for the foreshots (high in unwanted methanol), and one for the hearts (the ideal ethanol percentage for whisky), and one for the feints (high in fusel oils and sulfur). Assessors could measure the quality of each with a hydrometer, without contacting the liquid, by manipulating the spigot with an exterior crank-wheel. That arrangement kept the spirit safe from a distiller's meddling reach, keeping it secure until barreling.

In 1823, testing took place at the Excise Office in London. Aeneas Coffey, a young excise officer, suggested modifications and improvements to ensure that no one could access the liquid, including a lock with paper in the keyhole to reveal tampering. Robert Gottlieb patented that lock in 1829, much to Coffey's dismay, but four years later, Coffey patented his own device: the Coffey still.

These innovations created the spirit safe—as seen today in every distillery in Scotland and Ireland that uses pot stills—and the try box, its American equivalent. In 1852, *The Excise Officer's Manual* certified using a spirit safe for every distillery in Scotland. Officials installed them at Glenburgie, Linkwood, Miltonduff, and eventually at Port Ellen on Islay, the smuggler's paradise. It first featured the Gottlieb lock and later a double-keyed lock allowing it to be opened only by two keys at the same time, one in the possession of the distillery manager and the other held by the excise officer. Today, spirit safes remain unlocked because tax officials have more efficient ways to gauge output. Timing is everything, and in whisky, so are taxes.

Industrial Age

BEAM'S OLD TUB

IF YOU LOVE EUROPEAN HISTORY, YOU MAY SPEND YOUR FREE TIME tracing elaborate charts of the lineages of kings and queens, dukes and duchesses, and so on. Those charts have many downlines, broadening off the edges and hooking around in a complicated dance of boxes, lines, dotted lines, and a few circles. That attention to detail would serve you well when tracking the influence and heritage of the Jacob Beam family in Kentucky. It's not as long as that of European aristocracy, but the Beam heritage tells almost the entire story of whiskey in America.

Along with many others in American whiskey's history—the Bombergers, Shencks, Overholts—the Boehm family emigrated from the German Palatinate

region to Berks County, Pennsylvania, the epicenter of Amish, Mennonite, and Pennsylvania Dutch culture from the 1700s to the 1900s. The Boehms changed the family name to Beam and moved to Kentucky in 1792, the year that Congress enacted the whiskey tax and the Bluegrass State joined the Union. To encourage settlement, the federal government subsidized settlers with 60 acres to grow corn. The Beams joined a massive wave of Catholic emigrants from Maryland, including neighbor Elijah Craig, a frontier preacher. They all grew corn and distilled it. Patriarch Johannes "Jacob" Beam sold his first barrel of corn whiskey in 1795.

Jacob's son Jack created the Early Times brand, but we're turning our attention to his brother. In 1820, David Beam created the distillery that started the brand that proved the popularity of his father's whiskey. The distillery and whiskey shared the name Old Tub, which lasted until Prohibition took it down. After Repeal, Jeremiah Beam resurrected the distillery and renamed it and the now ubiquitous bourbon after his father, James Beauregard Beam. Since then, the Jim Beam brand has traveled a lot of miles. Ownership passed into the corporate hands of Seagram, then to the holding company American Brands, (renamed Fortune Brands). Distilling duties passed to Booker Noe, nephew of Jeremiah, the last of the Beams. Through whiskey's sour years, the brand—which in the company's portfolio shared space with golf balls, staplers, and faucets—continued to grow. In 2014, Suntory purchased Beam, which, through ten generations and counting, continues to dominate the whiskey landscape. Not quite the power or run of a royal family, but whiskey royalty nonetheless. The latest generations of Noes are still involved.

In 2020, Beam released a limited edition of Old Tub Bourbon, an unfiltered, 100 proof expression as close as possible to David Beam's old-line recipe.

FLAGGING THE CARDHU

THE 1823 EXCISE ACT LEGITIMIZED DISTILLATION IN BRITAIN. BUT paying the king's tax, as George Smith of Glenlivet parish had done, meant soldiers would be garrisoned in the area to protect the king's money, and those soldiers could find and destroy illicit stills. In Cardow, Scotland, Helen Cumming—matriarch of her family, unsung heroine of these transition days, and a profile in courage—had mastered the art of the switcheroo, often masquerading her kitchen distillations by covering herself with flour when the gaugers arrived and complaining that they were interrupting her bread baking. At other times, she invited them in and cooked them a meal. While they relaxed, she slipped outside to raise a red flag on a pole to warn neighbors of their presence. When the gaugers offered her a bribe to cooperate, she conspired with neighbors to place old, worn-out still parts behind the barn. The gaugers' "discovery" resulted in her fee, which she gladly split with her fellow distillers.

Industrial Age

The Cummings's distillery eventually became embroiled in another scandal that changed the labeling laws in Scotland. In the late 1800s, John Walker & Son purchased it to produce the key malt for its line of blended whiskies. As we jump into the 1900s and over the hump of World War II, Cardow whisky shipped to key European markets, including Spain, bottled as a single malt. Along the way, its spelling changed from Cardow to Cardhu, the old Scottish word for "black rock."

Then, in the 21st century, corporate owner Diageo committed the silliest misstep with long-ranging aftereffects. Running out of aged Cardhu malt to ship to Spain, they combined it with malts from their Glendullan distillery and labeled it "pure malt." Decades earlier, that designation had lost favor and legal standing. In the world of single malts, neither Cardhu nor Glendullan had a meaningful reputation, so apparently Diageo figured that they could slip this switcheroo under the table and move on. Spanish consumers may not have noticed, but the whisky industry cried foul, alleging that this mixing of malts could lead to an unbalanced trade advantage, given the number of malt distilleries that Diageo owned.

The resulting agitation led, in 2009, to a revision of the Scotch Whisky Regulations, the first revision since 1980. It formulated the five categories of Scotch that we use now: single malt, single grain, blended scotch, blended malt, and blended grain—you know, because it wasn't confusing enough already. So cover yourself in baking powder and raise a glass of Cardhu 12-year single malt while Helen Cumming raises her red flag for us.

CAMERONBRIDGE

BY THE END OF THE 1700S, THE STEINS AND HAIGS HAD CREATED THE world's first distilling dynasties. Between the families, they installed the first Boulton and Watt steam engines and created an export market with their own fleet of ships, and at one point, taxes on their combined output supported the crown's Exchequer. As in Canada and America before Prohibition, whisky paid almost all the taxes.

Those taxes allowed for the creation of railways that surged into the Highlands. The Haigs and Steins controlled the Lowlands market, but the railways gave the malt distilleries tucked into Highland glens a route to market. So they formed an alliance with distilleries in Northern England, jointly capturing the export market on cheap liquor rectified into gin, flooding London with it.

James, William, and Robert Haig each built distilleries in the Lowlands, as well. All told, the Steins and Haigs owned 13 Lowland distilleries with another two in Ireland. John Haig took over from his brother at Lochrin and bought two more distilleries in Leith and Cameron Bridge (town). Coffey stills joined the single-column still at Cameronbridge (distillery), credited as Scotland's largest and longest continuously running distillery. Today, gigantic, modern column stills have replaced the old stills to make most of the grain whisky for the Johnnie Walker blends, plus the neutral spirit for Gordon's and Tanqueray gin.

John Haig became the ringleader of the Scottish Distillers Association, which, in 1877, evolved into the Distillers Company Ltd. (DCL). The era of whisky barons had come, with a group of Lowland grain distillers known as the Big Five trying to control a quickly saturated market for grain spirits. Among them, they controlled more than 75 percent of grain spirits production. DCL eventually became today's Diageo.

In 1888, John's four sons created Haig & Haig Blended Scotch Whisky

Industrial Age

primarily for the American market, moving it into its Dimple bottle in 1893. Their exclusive American importer was Somerset Imports, owned by Joe Kennedy, father of the president. In 1952, that bottle design received a trademark from the US Patent Office, the first ever to qualify. Today we know that Haig brand as Pinch, a blended Scotch whisky with primary malts from the Glenkinchie and Linkwood distilleries and grain whisky from Cameronbridge.

SMITH'S GLENLIVET

If you're reading this book in chronological order, the focus on taxes may sound like a broken record, but they have more to do with whiskey's flavor than any other factor. Why? It's in a government's best interests to consolidate illicit activity into smaller, more efficient corporate units and to control it by taxation. It's in the best interests of the people being taxed to avoid it by changing their methods. In the middle, flavors emerge.

In 1644, England's Parliament imposed the first excise tax on whiskey to pay for the first English Civil War. Illicit distilling continued to grow, but in 1707, the Act of Union allowed English gaugers to cross the border into Scotland to levy a tax on every illicit still. This act probably spurred more distilling than any other because the Scots then claimed a birthright to make whisky. In 1713, a malt tax spurred the Malt Riots but more importantly affected the flavor of whisky. Lowlanders paid the tax on the malted portion, so they filled their pots mostly with treacle and unmalted grain to keep the tax rate low. The quality of the whisky grew so bad—"rascally," the poet Robert Burns called it—that it mostly went to England for redistillation into gin. But defiant Highlanders stuck to 100 percent malted barley while evading the tax, producing a better-tasting spirit.

In the mid-1700s, Scotland had an estimated 14,000 illegal stills. In 1784, the Wash Act formally separated the Highlands and Lowlands, imposing a tax on the capacity of a still and the estimated amount of whisky that it could produce in a certain amount of time. Highlanders engineered ways to speed the distillation process to short-circuit those calculations. The Duties on Spirits (Scotland) Act of 1814 set a five-hundred-gallon minimum for the Highlands with the idea that it would be difficult to move around and hide the required machinery, but the law inadvertently produced better-tasting whisky.

America's Whiskey Rebellion in the 1790s had spurred debate in Parliament, which passed the Excise Act of 1823 under the sponsorship of Alexander Gordon, 4th Duke of Gordon, a large landowner. The lords and representatives reasoned that no one could stop Highlanders from making whisky, so they might as well allow them to turn it into a profitable business that required a license. As the quality went up, they would tax the output as with any other commercial commodity.

George Smith worked as a tenant farmer, or crofter, on Gordon's estate, through which the River Spey flowed. By way of the duke, Smith's whisky had gained the favor of King George IV. After the 1823 Excise Act, Smith legitimized his operation in Glenlivet by buying one of the first licenses. Neighbors considered Smith a traitor in league with the crown, though, no longer a trusted co-conspirator and smuggler. As a result, Smith came under threats of violence and required a 24-hour security guard to protect his distillery and family. It prompted James Gordon, from the neighboring town of Aberlour, to gift Smith a pair of flintlock dueling pistols for protection. In 1824, George Smith rebuilt his now legal stills and produced Smith's Glenlivet, which expedited the birth of Speyside, the spiritual center of Highland malt. So we toast him and the tax collector with a bottle of The Glenlivet 15 Year Old.

Industrial Age

CHARCOAL FILTRATION

DON'T LET THE WORD *DISTILL* FOOL YOU. IT HAS SEVERAL DEFINITIONS. According to Webster, it means "to let fall, exude, or precipitate in drops or in a wet mist." Aboard a ship, Aristotle distilled seawater soaked into a large sponge suspended above a bucket. The sun, gravity, and the ship's movements drove fresh water from the sponge, leaving behind the salts and minerals. Distillation. Another definition reads: "to purify or transform (a liquid) by successive evaporation and condensation." In a cucurbit or bowl, soak an organic substance in liquid and allow the air to steal the liquid along with some of the matter. The condensate remains, a form of matter changed from the original. Distillation.

The charcoal filtration used in the Lincoln County Process represents another form of distillation. For preparing food and elixirs, ancient Egyptians filtered var-

ious substances through cloth, wool, stones, coal, and charred wood. They applied charcoal to festering wounds to filter the smell. Around 400 B.C.E., Phoenicians were using charred barrels to store water on long sea journeys to improve its taste. From 1785, we have documentary evidence of refined charcoal filtration used in St. Petersburg, Russia, creating a clear distillate. In the whiskey trade, the Scots and Irish used it to remove the harshness from the grain distillate that passed once through a copper still and still retained the dangerous methanol compound. Through the 1800s, Ontario distillers used charcoal separations in a multichambered still.

The tradition found a home with distillers in Robertson County, on Tennessee's border with Kentucky, as a less expensive way to "sweeten" the liquor, according to an 1887 Congressional report. Robertson County whiskey faded away, but across the state on the Alabama border, a small distillery called Jack Daniel was using the similar Lincoln County Process to make a finished whiskey as good as bourbon. Reportedly, it was taught to Jack by his mentor, a former slave named Nearest Green. By the time Brown-Forman acquired Jack Daniel in the 1970s, it had developed the process it uses today: whiskey poured over 10 feet of tightly packed lumps of charcoal made from burning ricks of dried sugar maple trees. It takes two and a half days for the whiskey to trickle through to the bottom of the tank. At Cascade Hollow, where the George Dickel brand began, the whiskey steeps in tanks of charcoal for about a week before draining. In 2013, Tennessee enacted a law that mandates charcoal filtration for any whiskey that carries the "Tennessee whiskey" designation on its label (with Benjamin Prichard's Tennessee Whiskey being the sole exception). But no single person can take credit for inventing charcoal filtration because the process is older than whiskey itself.

CROW'S SOUR MASH

JIM BEAM AND JACK DANIEL INCLUDE THE PHRASE "SOUR MASH" ON their labels, a brilliant marketing move akin to advertising a new automobile that comes *with* a windshield. They're not saying that others *don't* have one, but . . .

In the early frontier days, a wooden mash tun or fermenting tub likely did double duty as a wash tub or storage vessel. Bacteria was unknown to the average settler, so a quick rinse or salt rub of the tub between uses would have been the standard procedure. After grinding corn, it soaks in hot water in the tub to leach the sugar from within. Not completely sterilizing the tub between uses invites leftovers from the last contents to make their home within the cracks and pores of the tub's slats, effectively spoiling it for distillation purposes.

Born in Inverness, Scotland, James C. Crow studied medicine at the University of Edinburgh and immigrated to America around 1814. From New York, he moved to Philadelphia and by about 1825 moved again to Kentucky. At that time, America was awash in whiskey, most of it bad. Trained as a chemist and physician, he worked as an itinerant distiller, encountering various folk remedies used to cure the mash—with inconsistent results. Crow receives credit for introducing stringent scientific methodology to ensure mash consistency for his clients, including Oscar Pepper and E. H. Taylor.

In the hot, humid conditions of Kentucky, Crow understood that the pH level of the mash tended toward highly alkaline, meaning that it lacked acid. One popular remedy was to add a portion of spent mash from a previous distillation to the next mash, much like a "mother" with sourdough bread. Devoid of all sugar and alcohol, the fresh mash was called "soured," and it raised the acid level of the mash, not only bringing it in balance but also ensuring consistency from batch to batch.

    As America's distilling operations were moving from the East Coast to the frontier and beyond—with western Kentucky, on the Ohio River, as the new epicenter—Crow found himself in the right place at the right time. Oscar Pepper recognized Crow's brilliance and talent and brought him on as a partner.

    Crow died in 1856 with no heirs. In 1868, W. A. Gaines and Co. bought Crow's old stock, leased Oscar Pepper's distillery, and hired Crow's former assistant to distill for them. They trademarked Old Crow Whiskey in 1870. For the next one hundred plus years, the rights to Old Crow's name passed from company to company, brand to brand. The sour-mash process had become the de facto preparation for bourbon and whiskey from that region. The cartoon crow on the label reportedly represents a compromise between the Confederacy and Union so that it could be shipped north after the Civil War. In 1987, Beam bought Old Crow, relocated production, dumbed down the mash bill, changed the formulation, and gutted the once celebrated brand, an ignominious salute to the man who laid the foundation for bourbon to become what it is today. Hopefully clearer minds will prevail and revive a version worthy of the name on the label.

Industrial Age

COFFEY STILL

SINCE THE FIRST DAYS OF THE POT-STILL ALEMBIC, HUMANITY FACED an irascible vice while using it: impatience. All that standing around waiting for *distillare,* the drip from a pipe while watching the tick of the clock. It was maddening.

For most of its history, distillation was a spiritual path toward unification and purification of the four elements of the universe: earth, wind, fire, and water. But as artisanal production gave way to industrialism, an idea emerged: more and better output for less work. If distillation is purification, then the more we distill a thing, the purer the result. Industry and economics were working hand in hand to shape the future of whiskey as the pot was about to transform into a column.

The list of French patents granted in the 1700s and 1800s reads like a who's who of distilling wine into brandy or pure chemical experimentation. Starting in the 1700s, we encounter the separation bottles of Peter Woulfe and Angelo Saluzzo; then Antoine Lavoisier, father of modern chemistry, who demonstrated their scientific application. In 1801, we get serious with patents going to the real pioneers: Edouard Adam, Laurent Solimani, and J. B. Fornier. Isaac Berard made improvements, and Jean-Antoine Chaptal combined everything in a proper laboratory setting.

Jean-Baptiste Cellier-Blumenthal, a hitherto unknown player, synthesized and patented it all. The simple alembic was stretched, mounted on itself, and doubled back again, subject to fractionating and multiple condensations. Cellier-Blumenthal didn't want to make brandy or any form of aqua vitae, though. He was trying to manufacture sugar from sugar beets. His innovation importantly replaced the manually intensive, time-consuming batch distillation of the alembic with the first continuously operating distillation column.

The next leap is critical. Across the English Channel, we return to a member of the first family of Scotland's Lowland distillers: the Steins. Robert Stein grabbed Cellier-Blumenthal's column and modified it for grain mash, using pistons to move the mash through heavy woolen separators. The idea was right, but the execution wasn't. The resulting alcohol ran thick with fusel oils and sludge and needed constant maintenance.

Enter our hero, Aeneas Coffey, from the most unlikely place: the excise booth at a Dublin distillery, where he worked as a taxman for 25 years. Coffey took Stein's single column and snapped it into two pieces, rectifier and analyzer, which he patented in 1830. It was continuous, self-cleaning, and sensed when all the alcohol had been stripped away. Revolutionary in every way, it eventually morphed into today's column still.

In the 1960s, Masataka Taketsuru, founder of Nikka Whisky Distilling, imported an original-model Coffey still from Scotland to his Miyagikyo distillery, which produces Coffey Grain Whisky. On the back label of the bottle, an illustration depicts the still, one of only four in the world. You can find the others in Canada and Scotland, where no one has to wait around like they used to.

USHER IN THE BLENDS

THOSE HAIGS WERE GOING TO BE A PROBLEM. ONCE A FAMILY BECOMES a dynasty, it tends to become a mafia, as well. The Haig and Stein families had acquired a few centuries of social and political influence before they started distilling in the 1600s. At the start of the Industrial Revolution, they expanded their operations at Kennetpans and Kilbagie. But their stills spewed out all manner of spirits made of anything they threw into it, with much of the result crossing the border to England for redistillation into gin. They meanwhile united around their Cameronbridge Distillery to control grain whisky pricing across Scotland. Something had to be done.

In the 1830s, Andrew Usher, a spirits dealer, acquired exclusive rights to blend and to sell George Smith's Glenlivet, one of the first licensed Highland distilleries. Usher and later his sons Andrew and John obtained rough-edged, smoky malts and, through their wizardry, transformed them into drinkable,

vatted malts. But an unfashionable, rough edge still lingered around the result. They brought in other blenders, such as William Sanderson of Vat 69 and John Watson, and formed the North British Distillery Company while Haig's Cameronbridge was struggling with Robert Stein's infernal one-column contraption. North British directly challenged the hegemony of the Distillers Company Ltd. (DCL), a new Haig-Stein company.

The Ushers immediately recognized the value of the Coffey still. Lighter grain whisky served as a neutral bed into which they could lay various distinctive malts, increasing the palate of flavors that they could produce, much like an artist uses white paint to increase a color's range. If Edinburgers liked it spicy, the Ushers could make a blend just for them. If Glaswegians loved smoke and fire, a different blend for them. For English palates accustomed to brandy and soda, something equally refined.

Inside and outside Scotland, Andrew and John Usher smartly expanded the drinking tastes of fashionable society beyond brandy and soda to Scotch whisky. After the devastation of phylloxera, Irish whiskey conquered France, but the Ushers upended that dominance. Dewar and Walker were ascending at the same time, but the Ushers' blending methodology has placed them at the top of the blender's hierarchy. Blenders today hold Andrew Jr., the father of modern whisky blending, as the original inspiration for their craft. As proof of Scotch's attractiveness, Usher's Old Vatted Glenlivet Whisky blend and, later, Usher's Green Stripe captured the loyalty of palates throughout Britain, Europe, America, and Japan. After the Usher brothers died, DCL absorbed the North British Distilling Company in 1919. DCL's descendent, Diageo, still owns North British today.

MOLSON DISTILLERY

EVERY STUDENT OF WHISKEY LEARNS THAT MIDWAY THROUGH THE process, from grain to glass, beer happens. Malt the grains, grind them, soak them in hot water, and add yeast to the mash. Beer results, which goes into the still for purification and separation, resulting in whiskey. In Scotland and Ireland, this beer is called the wash, a linguistic downgrade and kind of an insult.

From the eastern Canadian provinces, pioneers pushing westward on the 18th-century frontier knew about distilling. But it was complex, time-consuming, and manually intensive, so rum from the East Coast became the spirit of choice on the

Canadian prairie. After the American War of Independence, immigrants loyal to the crown fled north to Canada, bringing their brewing and distilling knowledge with them. Brewing signals that a community has come of age, that it has become a settled location with active trading. As in Europe, beer had a close association with good health and vitality. Being a cousin to bread, it was considered food. The Molson family's impact began here.

John Molson came from England to North America in 1782. His brewing activity began early, as a teenager, and after a few fits and starts, he built a significant operation. Molson's real distilling story begins with two of his sons, Thomas and William. Thomas Molson, the curious outlier, eventually licensed a still in 1821, and William Molson opened a distillery in 1833. By 1836, they had reached 31,000 gallons of salable product. Among the proliferation of small farm distilleries, they were attaining industrial scale in Canada. By 1845, production had peaked at 250,000 gallons, most of it exported to England.

Then the bottom dropped out of the English market. In Scotland, railways opened a route from Highland distillers to the blenders in the Lowlands, creating a new industry there. Closer to home, Canadian competitors, including Gooderham & Worts, J. P. Wiser, and Hiram Walker, got in on the action. Thomas Molson's son John inherited the business but saw the writing on the wall. As taxes on distilled spirits rose and sales leveled off, he consolidated the distillery into the brewery. It was a good run, and it proved that whisky could be distilled at scale in Canada—just not with the Molson name attached to it. So pop the top of a frosty bottle of Molson Golden to remind yourself why beer and whisky go so well together.

VICTORIAN ERA

"MEN INTO SWINE"

AUSTRALIA'S HISTORY WITH PROHIBITION LOOKS JUST AS SCHIZOphrenic as other Western countries. Founded in 1788 as a result of Britain losing its American colonies, Australia also began as separate colonies, each with its own alcohol laws. In 1822, distillation appeared in Hobart, a port town and the capital of Van Diemen's Land, now Tasmania. By 1830, residents there reportedly were drinking five times more than the British. In the convict period, which lasted until 1868, the region teemed with single men, and rum served as a legitimate currency, boosting the land's reputation for drunken lawlessness.

At the same time, the temperance movement washed ashore like a tsunami, first in Van Diemen's Land, then through the eastern states. The governor of New South Wales stopped the daily tot of rum for local troops while imposing an excise tax. As in Britain and America, temperance grew with the establishment of local branches of the Woman's Christian Temperance Union, the restriction of local licenses, and excise taxes. It peaked in 1838, when Jane, Lady Franklin, wife of the lieutenant-governor of Van Diemen's Land, declared: "I would prefer barley be fed to pigs than it be used to turn men into swine." The Distillation Prohibition Act of 1839 followed. That ban lasted for only eight years, but it had a chilling effect for more than a century. In 1901, Australia's states federated, with new laws emphasizing the industrialization of alcohol output. They set the minimum still size at 2,700 liters, or 713 gallons. That minimum invigorated the fortified wine industry, but whisky startups were now out of the question.

In 1989, Bill Lark was sharing a bottle of single malt Scotch while trout fishing and wondered: "Why isn't anyone mak-

Jane Griffin (later Lady Franklin) in 1816 by Amélie Munier-Romilly

ing malt whisky in Tasmania?" On a whim, he visited a local legislator's office to ask about the still size regulation, which favored large industrial distilling. This innocent inquiry unwittingly led to its reversal, launching Australia's whisky renaissance. Using a one-gallon still purchased for $65, Bill and Lyn Lark produced a single malt at their kitchen table that they released in 1992, the first from Tasmania in more than 150 years. Now run by their daughter, the Lark Distillery has received international acclaim, and output exceeds 300,000 liters per year.

At the same time, Brian and Fay Poke, another husband-and-wife team, began a similar journey. Their distillery, now called Cradle Mountain Distillery, and currently operated by different owners, releases aged whiskies to worldwide applause. With the establishment of Sullivans Cove Distillery in 1994, Tasmania became the unlikely epicenter of the Australian malt whisky revival.

The Australian reawakening culminated in 2007, with Starward in Melbourne. Owner David Vitale took inspiration from Lark's advocacy for smaller still regulations and his approach to making Scottish-style whisky in Tasmania. Starward Nova takes Scotch as its starting point, making malt whisky in pot stills but then aging it in "wet" barrels gathered from surrounding Australian vineyards. In doing so, Vitale not only created a distinctive flavor profile very much of that area of the world, but he's showing the three hundred or so other distilleries across the country how to leverage tradition for the next one hundred years while denying pigs their barley.

Victorian Era

THE BOOZ LOG CABIN DECANTER

DRINKING GAMES ARE FUN. OPEN A BOTTLE OF WHISKEY, TAKE A SIP, and slide down the rabbit hole of how whiskey got its name. A millennium ago, Latinate monks called hard alcohol *aqua vitae,* which in English is "water of life." In French, that became *eau de vie* and, in Slavic languages, *voda* (meaning "little water") that evolved to *vodka*). In Irish Gaelic, it took the form of *uisce beatha,* and the Scottish form, *uisge beatha,* morphed into *uskebeaghe,* then *iskie bae,* and eventually whisky. It's a great little linguistic journey to take after the third glass with friends.

"Booze" is more direct but just as fun. Its root, *bous,* has been around since the 1500s, meaning some form of drink or a drinking vessel. But a historical coincidence most likely spread its popularity. If Edmund G. Booz were alive today, he'd be number one on your invite list and the life of any party. In 1824, Booz was born in Bucks County, Pennsylvania, the center of rye whiskey production in America. He imported and sold alcoholic beverages such as wine, brandy, Madeira, port, and other high-end libations that catered to the blue-blood patronage of Philadelphia. Distilleries, vineyards, bodegas, and breweries then didn't have the same presence as the commercial entities of today. In the 1700s and 1800s, the merchant, distributor, or tavern was more likely to put its brand—or mark—on the barrel containing the drink. Drinkers associated that name with what they carried home and enjoyed.

President William Harrison

The last American president born as a British subject, William Harrison, won the 1840 presidential election in part by using a log cabin as a campaign symbol to differentiate himself from Martin Van Buren, his aristocratic competitor. Harrison died in office just 31 days after his inauguration, making him the first president to die in office and his presidency the shortest in American history. A decade after the election, Booz created a glass decanter shaped like a log cabin, because log-cabin sentiment still ran high. That move cemented Booz's name for all time. Booz embossed his own name and "1840" on the piece, a maker's mark and hallmark of his growing business that lasted until his death in 1870.

Jumping ahead into the mid-1900s, distilleries across the globe were releasing their brands in ornate, decorated decanters as a form of promotion. In the 1950s, E. G. Booz Distillery Company of Bardstown, Kentucky, and later Boston, revived the Booz brand. An enterprising company, they commissioned a series of bottles, log cabins and regular, with Booz's name on them, which they filled with Kentucky Straight Bourbon Whiskey. We can rest assured that Booz, in every form, always lies within reach because, as the Bardstown company reminded us: "It's a name so famous it became part of the English language."

Victorian Era

CADENHEAD'S INDEPENDENT BOTTLING

HERE'S A HYPOTHETICAL: A MAN MAKES A CONSUMABLE PRODUCT that generates a local fan base, but he lives in a tiny village in the mountains and only a lucky few know about it. The product is flavorful, but because it's a side job, it's somewhat inconsistent and definitely "regional" in flavor. Faraway merchants could use it to blend with other similar products to make something unique for their customers. But they have no knowledge of this producer due to the distance between them. A producer with no path to market and a marketer with no access to raw goods—enter the middleman and welcome to Scotch whisky in the 1800s.

From deep in the glens of the Highlands, middlemen were the logistical link that brought the work of malt distilleries to the merchants, blenders, and bottling houses of Aberdeen, Glasgow, and Edinburgh.

Sometimes these middlemen smuggled it or, as entrepreneurs, provided a legitimate service. They had buckboard wagons, horses, and the knowledge of how to navigate treacherous Highland passes, or they had the wherewithal to book passage on ships from Inverness to Aberdeen. By the mid-1850s, railways were streaming from Lowland port cities into the Highlands. The middlemen purchased barrels of whisky and had to sell them at a profit or lose their investment. As their operations became more sophisticated, they bought or built warehouses to hold or transfer those barrels. For some, this structure offered an opportunity to sell directly to consumers by opening a shop in the front.

This arrangement allowed for the rise of independent bottlers in Britain, who

often combined logistics, wholesale, and retail into one effort. In the Highlands, Gordon & MacPhail started as a grocery store, added local malts to their inventory of coffee and teas, sold direct from the cask, and blended them, as well. Eventually, instead of purchasing barrels from distilleries, they placed fill orders with them, supplying their own barrels and maturing them in their own warehouses. In London, Berry Brothers & Rudd imported and sold whiskies, wines, sherries, and ports. Their first records of bottling alcohol date to 1780, and they started selling their own blended spirits in 1803.

In Scotland, the number of independent bottlers and brokers has become legion. Cadenhead's, the oldest, started in 1842 as a wine and spirits shop in Aberdeen. It passed through many hands, from William Cadenhead to the J. A. Mitchell firm, owners of Springbank Distillery in Campbeltown. Here, you can find single-cask bottlings from well-known distilleries along with obscure producers who sell directly to blenders in bulk. Cadenhead's shelves contain a treasure trove of liquid history, recalling a time when barrels traveled overland or by sea for consumers just like you.

NELSON'S GREEN BRIER TENNESSEE WHISKEY

MANY OF THE FAMOUS NAMES OF WHISKEY STARTED AS MERCHANTS. They sold commodities, such as dry goods, bakery items, meats, oil, fish, and tools. Discriminating merchants sought the best teas, coffees, wines, and fortified wines such as sherry, port, and Madeira. Larger establishments traded in livestock, horses, and farm equipment. Practically all of them sold whiskey in one form or another, mostly rectifying sourced spirits to suit their needs. Here's a short list of familiar whiskey brands that began in the merchant business.

- SCOTLAND: Cadenhead's, Chivas Brothers, John Dewar & Son, Gordon & MacPhail, John Walker & Son
- CANADA: Henry Corby, Hiram Walker
- IRELAND: Mitchell & Son (Spot)
- ENGLAND: Berry Brothers & Rudd (Cutty Sark)
- JAPAN: Torii Shoten (Suntory)

Sometimes, history loses track of a name, never to be heard again unless a lucky break happens. In 1850, Charles Nelson and his family arrived, penniless, from northern Germany to New York. He settled later in Cincinnati, a great place to learn how to become a butcher and how to rectify and sell whiskey. Before the Civil War, he moved to Nashville, set up shop, and sold meats, coffee, and whiskey purchased from a nearby distillery in Greenbrier, Tennessee. Whiskey soon became his most popular product. He purchased the distillery, expanded production, and was selling Green Brier Tennessee Whiskey in markets as far as the Philippines.

But Prohibition in Tennessee, a Bible Belt state, took effect in 1909, a decade ahead of the rest of the country, and spelled the end of Nelson's whiskey.

Jump to 2006, when brothers Charles and Andrew Nelson stepped into a butcher shop in Greenbrier, near where they grew up, and chatted with the butcher about rumors of their thrice-great-grandfather's business. "Look across the street over there," the butcher said. "Your granddaddy built that warehouse. This street is Distillery Road, you know."

Within three years, the brothers launched Belle Meade, a sourced brand named after one of their ancestor's products. In 2019, they bottled their first Nelson Brothers Classic Bourbon from their own distillery. That brand now owned by Constellation Brands, sells well across all markets, as far as the Philippines, proving that one should never pass up an opportunity to chat up a local retailer to unlock local secrets.

UNCLE NEAREST AND JACK DANIEL

IT WAS SINATRA'S DRINK. EVERY BIKER BAR AND ROADHOUSE JOINT across the country carries it. Out-of-control rock stars careening from trashed-out hotel rooms to backstage at the Fillmore swilled it. If you open a bar—whether the Ritz-Carlton or the Sportsman's Club—you stock it first. Its iconic shape and black label proclaiming "Old No. 7" and "Tennessee Sour Mash Whiskey" have imprinted on your temporal lobe. It defined whiskey for two generations of drinkers, no matter their station, from college campuses to private homes. It's Jack Daniel's, dammit, and admit it: You drank it.

Was Jack Daniel a real person? Who knew? Who cared? Well, that apathy came from before the internet opened the story; and yes, he was a real person who

Victorian Era

made his whiskey in Lynchburg, a famously dry town in Tennessee—just like the label says. Clear limestone water flows in the creek near the massive facility that makes it. Famous distillers distill it and run it through ricks of charred sugar maple ground to perfect charcoal bits to filter it. Here, they tell the story of Jack Daniel, dapper Southern gent dressed in his Edwardian coat and hat. From a local distiller, he learned his trade as an orphan and built his own distillery. They show the iron safe in his office where, in a fit of anger over a government ruling, Daniel kicked the door and severely injured a toe, which got infected and led to his death. With that special American blend of attitude and perseverance, he "invented" whiskey in America. Here, Jack Daniel came alive; here, he became a real person. But we didn't get the whole story.

In 2016, *The New York Times* published a story revealing the man who taught Daniel how to distill. The article ran a photo from the era, showing Daniel seated next to a Black man, George Green, son of Nathan Green. Nathan, a recently freed slave, worked as head distiller at the distillery where Daniel apprenticed as a youngster. The story caught the interest of entrepreneur Fawn Weaver, and "interest" may be an understatement. It lit a fire under her, fueling an obsession to find out more about this man ignored by history. In her research, she reportedly accumulated nearly ten thousand documents and artifacts associated with Nathan Green that brought him back to life.

Daniel himself kept meticulous records showing that Nathan Green and his sons received wages as fair as any of the white men in his employ. Weaver met members of Nathan's family, down the generations, and found that, across two centuries, a member of the Green family was always working at the Jack Daniel Distillery. She learned that the relationship between the men consisted of more than just turning corn

George Green, son of Nathan Green, a.k.a. Uncle Nearest, on left, and Jack Daniel on right.

into whiskey. Nathan Green served as a sort of mentor to the orphaned young man. To Jack, he was Uncle Nearest. After the Civil War, in the Reconstructionist South, Green family lore kept the knowledge of this unusual relationship alive.

It became clear to Weaver what she had to do: create a whiskey to honor the first known Black man to distill whiskey in the 1800s. She and her husband, Keith, an executive at Sony, created Uncle Nearest Premium Whiskey, and fittingly they brought in Victoria Eady Butler, Nathan's great-great granddaughter, to blend it. They gathered hand-chosen barrels of aged whiskey from other distilleries and blended them in the style of that era, using 10 feet of charcoal to filter it. In 2017, they launched Uncle Nearest 1856, which has accrued multiple awards.

But that was only the beginning. They built an expansive, new distillery to ensure that making the whiskey continued to honor Green's memory by attracting visitors from around the world. An accelerator program supports and teaches young people of color the mechanics and art of distilling and maturation. A fund-raising program for historically Black colleges and universities provides tuition to each accredited school. The list goes on.

For decades, Jack Daniel's has ranked as one of the top-selling spirit brands in the world. Fawn Weaver's limitless vision promises that, 175 years later, the gap between Jack Daniel and Nathan Green may close, allowing them one day to make whiskey side-by-side again.

Victorian Era

GOODERHAM, WORTS, AND CANADIAN INDUSTRIALIZATION

I N THE MID-1800S, THE AMERICAN WHISKEY TRADE FOCUSED ON PENNsylvania and Maryland, with a few small startups in Kentucky. Scotland's DCL had yet to aggregate into the forcefield of power that it became. Dublin's Big Four—Jameson (John and William), Power, and Roe—had the best shot at a style monopoly. But once the combined power of Gooderham & Worts, Walker, Seagram, Corby, and Wiser took the stage, North American whiskey got its first taste of industrialization. On a map, their Canadian distilling operations formed an offensive line that stretched from Lake Michigan to the tip of Lake Ontario.

In 1831, James Worts emigrated from England to Canada, soon followed by his brother-in-law William Gooderham. They set up grain mills as they had in their birth country. In 1834, after the death of his wife in childbirth, Worts took his own life. Gooderham expanded operations to rectifying, using columns of charcoal to sweeten pot-still spirits from approximately 150 distilleries in Ontario. His first

"still" was a box of stones, with steam pumped from the bottom and beer from the top. The surface of the rocks provided the transfer point where the alcohol was stripped, a crude precursor to the plates in today's column still. They were the first to experiment with the wooden version of the three-chamber still that Todd Leopold currently revived in Colorado. They adopted an updated form of the Coffey still, called the Riley Patent. James Riley and William Allen had modified Coffey's still for distilling rosin oil, patenting it in 1853. But the Gooderhams saw in it key competitive elements for whisky making: efficiency and yield.

In 1856, they expanded their distillery, adding large pot stills and 42 large rectifying columns holding charcoal. This was roughly the same time as distilleries in Robertson and Lincoln counties in Tennessee using

similar techniques. Steam powered the entire operation. The disruption of the American Civil War helped move their whiskey deep into the United States and elsewhere. At one time, they ranked as the largest distillery in the world, producing more than 2 million gallons of whisky that was exported across the globe. At the end of the 1800s, they served as the largest source of revenue for Toronto *and* Canada. But that growth brought ill-effects.

In 1890, the world's first minimum aging law—initially one year, later expanded to two and then three years—codified the quality of Canadian whisky but dented the bottom line. The 20th century wasn't kind, either. Tightening excise controls by the Canadian government further eroded profitability. Whisky entrepreneur Harry Hatch eventually acquired Gooderham & Worts, merging it with Hiram Walker during the American Prohibition.

Gooderham & Worts Four Grain Whisky, produced today at the Hiram Walker plant in Windsor, Ontario, pays homage to distilling the middlings, a mix of all grain types that farmers used to pay millers. Four-grain whiskies are a rarity today, so consider each sip a tiny blast from Canada's industrial past.

VAT 69

BRANDS LOVE A FIRST—AS IN, "WE WERE THE FIRST TO USE HORSE dung to heat our alembics." OK, that may have been a little alchemical bragging from a 12th-century monk, but you get the point. The other point is that the history of whiskey suffers from the fog of memory. Two world wars and Prohibition practically shot a cannonball through the entire industry, sinking the institutional memory that served as its underpinning. In many cases, we suffer from global whiskey amnesia. From the 1970s to the 1990s, industry fortunes dipped again, but today's computers and smartphones mean that arcane trivia, factoids, and firsts prove less likely to slip through our fingers without notice.

One of those firsts happened in the 1800s, when empty sherry casks lay strewn on the docks of Edinburgh and Leith like empty cups on today's roads. They originated in Spain, in the bodegas of Jerez (which English speakers mangled into *Sherry*). The negotiants who imported the Spanish fortified wine filled the empties with whiskies bought from local distilleries, birthing a new style: sherry-flavored whisky. Thankfully we have documentation of the first use of a sherry barrel to mature whisky. In 1854, William Sanderson, a Scottish blender, was creating a blend and noted the effects of an ex-sherry barrel on its taste. He used a host of solid methodologies to create his formulas, including tasting panels and blind evaluations. He lined up 100 "vattings" of his blend and, over a period of days, set his panel to evaluate them. They unanimously favored vat #69, a brand still sold today as Vat 69. In 1880, Mackenzie Whisky, which owned the Dalmore

Distillery, followed with a 12-year malt racked into Sherrywood and bottled it in 1891. Dalmore continues its sherry association today.

After World War II, sherry consumption declined at the same time that America adopted new regulations mandating charred new oak containers for aging bourbon. Suddenly, a huge secondary market for these used barrels opened. Scotland had no such restriction on barrel usage, so the taste of Scotch whisky began its next flavor shift, dominated by ex-bourbon barrels. Today, they account for an estimated 94 percent of aging whisky stock.

Dalmore's Richard Paterson keeps his relationship with González Byass, a bodega in Jerez, tight and personal. He and Antonio Flores y Silvia of González Byass, both masters of their art, collaborated on Nomad Outland Whisky. They make the blend with a selection of more than 30 malt and grain whiskies aged for six years in Scotland. Then it ships to Jerez, where it finishes in ex–Pedro Ximénez casks for a year before bottling. Now that's a first.

WALKERVILLE

HIRAM WALKER, THE NAME THAT MOST PEOPLE ASSOCIATE WITH Canadian whisky, ironically was born in Massachusetts. In 1838, as a young man, he moved to Detroit, a boom town bustling with fur trading, farming, and manufacturing. In 1848, Walker opened a grocery store that distilled vinegar, traded in commodities, and shipped grains and leather products. He also blended and leached out bad flavors from the local moonshine. A good merchant pleases his customers.

His business acumen led him across the Detroit River to Windsor, Ontario. The western extension of the Great Western Railway activated his ambitions for a purpose-built distillery and access to far-off markets, much like his Scottish counterparts of the same era. At the Detroit grocery, his first distillations took place in a pot still, using charcoal as a rectifier, similar to other Canadian and

Distillery buildings in Walkerville, Ontario

Tennessee distillers. But his new parcel of Canadian land, almost five hundred acres, provided him with the opportunity to expand his operations in a country with lower taxes and cheaper grain. Additionally, the hot specter of temperance wasn't breathing down his neck.

Along with an expanded distilling operation, he built an ecosystem around it: Walkerville. It housed his workers and served as the model of a factory town with its own electrical plant, sewage system, and fire department. He incorporated grain mills for local farmers who supplied his mash bill, and cattle and hog farms to consume the stillage. He first brought in "big copper," a three-chamber still and copper doublers with charcoal rectifiers. Then the upgrade: A version of the Coffey still that increased output tenfold. Being so close to America's grain enabled him to buy corn more cheaply than his competitors, which gave him a price advantage.

The whisky that made his name came in 1879. Delicate and smooth, it became the favorite of gentlemen's clubs across Canada, America, and Britain, and eventually was marketed as Club Whisky. Excise laws in America and Canada were changing, allowing Walker to include the country of origin on the label, so the name changed to Canadian Club (CC). Initially sold in five-gallon ceramic crocks, the familiar brown bottle appeared in 1880, and in 1898, CC received its royal warrant from Queen Victoria. The mash bill never changed, though: primarily corn distilled twice through a column, with rye and malt distilled once through a column and pot still.

Walker's distillery remains active in Windsor, making numerous Canadian brands. But irony also remains a cornerstone of the Hiram Walker story. Pernod Ricard, a French company, owns the distillery, and Suntory Holdings of Japan owns the Canadian Club brand. Your CC and ginger has quite the global heritage.

THE WHISKEY RING, PACS AMERICANA

DURING ANDREW JOHNSON'S PARTIAL TERM AS PRESIDENT, ST. LOUIS distillers created it as a Republican fundraiser. In 1870, it was reignited for Ulysses Grant, Johnson's Republican successor in office, with an expanded scope that made it "coextensive" with the American government to advance the interests of GOP candidates. After Grant's reelection, it made everyone rich, a government-based slush fund designed to defraud the government. "It" was the Whiskey Ring, the first political action committee (PAC). At the center stood John McDonald, a former general appointed by Grant as Internal Revenue collector for the Missouri District.

At the end of the Civil War, as supply chains reformed, distillers found their legs again but still were struggling with Lincoln's wartime whiskey tax. One measurement for the tax used fermentation time for grain, set at 48 hours, which achieved the highest yield. For this purpose, the Bureau of Internal Revenue kept records

LEFT TO RIGHT: The inauguration of President Ulysses Grant (left), and the trial of Orville Babcock (right).

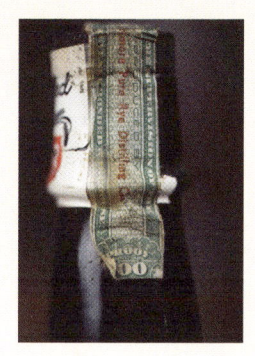  

detailing every filling and emptying of mash tuns, and of which grains, to determine output. In the Ring, crooked revenue agents sold the reports back to the distillers on Saturday nights for $10,000 each, giving them an opportunity to deflate their production numbers to evade taxes. They then sold the untaxed whiskey in underground marketplaces. Distillers, gaugers, and rectifiers all had to cooperate for the scheme to work. If someone didn't cooperate, they were extorted back in. If that didn't work, they went out of business.

This system wasn't "one ring to rule them all" but a network established in 16 cities, including St. Louis, Chicago, Milwaukee, and New Orleans. The *St. Louis Globe-Democrat* and German-language *Illinois Staats-Zeitung* in Chicago supported them as "anti-temperance" efforts. Milwaukee distillers had to pay $10,000 for "political purposes" to make "crooked whiskey, carte blanche" for the men running the local Ring, notable and "honorable businessmen" involved in the liquor and malting industries. In Chicago, Anton Hesing, a former sheriff and owner of the *Staats-Zeitung,* enabled a tax stamp clerk to steal books of stamps meant for distillers and sell them to local rectifiers. If distillers didn't cough up enough money to the Ring, the boss arranged for honest gaugers to expose them.

Grant launched an investigation and sicced Treasury Secretary Benjamin Bristow on the trail, only to fire him later. Grant discovered that Orville Babcock, his friend, personal secretary, and the top enabler, had betrayed him. A combination of Revenue and Treasury agents eventually broke the rings, which cost the American government more than $4 million in lost tax revenue over two years. Some 200 indictments and 110 convictions resulted, including McDonald, whom the court fined $5,000 and sentenced to serve 18 months in jail. President Grant pardoned McDonald, who was threatening to expose the entire affair and name names, after serving 17 months of his sentence. History repeats itself, but the reforms that followed the scandal remain in place today.

GOLDEN WEDDING PARTNERS

IF YOU TRACE THE PLAYERS AND BRANDS OF AMERICAN WHISKEY FROM the 1800s, through Prohibition, and into the 21st century, one keeps coming to the front as a narrative keystone: Joseph Finch's Golden Wedding Rye. It touched practically everyone and everything in the American whiskey world.

On the Monongahela River in Pittsburgh, Thomas Moore created Possum Hollow Rye, a whiskey that made a name for itself as far as New York City. Joseph Finch, his son-in-law, took over the operation from Moore, and he started his own enterprise in 1864. A few years later, Finch partnered with John Painter, and they called their business Joseph S. Finch & Company, building another new facility in 1868 and releasing Golden Wedding Pure Rye Pennsylvania Whiskey. In 1884, Finch died at age 44. James Pontefract, who had connections with the Overholt Distillery upriver and understood the power of marketing, bought into the company. Finch's Golden Wedding soon sprouted many successful variations, which the company trademarked. After Painter retired, Pontefract became sole owner of Finch & Company. Pontefract leased the entire enterprise to

Willis and R. G. Johnson. When they exited the business, Sol Rosenbloom bought it, then sold it in 1920 to Lewis Rosenstiel.

Next to Sam Bronfman of Seagram, there was no more powerful person in the liquor industry in the 1900s than Rosenstiel, and the two were bitter rivals. Under the banner of the Cincinnati Distributing Corporation, Rosenstiel purchased Finch's Pittsburgh distillery right before Prohibition. Rosenstiel owned the Schenley Distillery, one of six operations granted a medicinal license at the start of Prohibition.

He moved the Finch operation there but kept the name of the brand, which still had a strong market presence. In 1933, after Prohibition ended, Schenley Industries went public and soon became one of the four largest liquor companies in the world, alongside Seagram, National, and Hiram Walker.

Rosenstiel acquired a who's who of brands: James E. Pepper, I. W. Harper, Cream of Kentucky, George T. Stagg, and Squibb (right next to Bronfman's Rossville operation in Indiana). In the 1940s, Rosenstiel opened a distillery in Canada and moved the Golden Wedding brand there, reincarnating it as a three-year-old Canadian blend. His British subsidiary teamed up with DCL in Scotland and imported Guinness beer. Guinness had corporate ties to United Distillers, which owned Bernheim and Stitzel-Weller in Kentucky. In 1968, investor Meshulam Riklis bought Schenley and, in 1987, sold it back to United Distillers, amid financial scandal. That tradeoff eventually became today's Diageo.

Through it all, Golden Wedding survived iteration after iteration, but it kept slipping from shelf to shelf, ending up on the bottom as a cheap blend in a plastic bottle that Sazerac now owns. Golden Wedding reached its platinum anniversary before beginning its long, slow descent into obscurity, but with so many owners, it's amazing that it exists at all today.

Victorian Era

PRESCRIPTION IN A BOTTLE

THE LONG JOURNEY FROM AQUA VITAE FOR CURATIVE PURPOSES TO whiskey as a recreational drink left a historical marker in its DNA that still considers it "medicine." Nowadays, that descriptor comes with a wink, but tradition still calls for Hot Toddies in winter and Scotch 'n' Milk for "ulcers." Alcohol is, after all, an antiseptic and an anesthetic.

In the 1800s, doctors prescribed it, but no laws guaranteed its purity. George Garvin Brown, a pharmaceutical salesman, understood whiskey's dual use. He also knew the route to market of a distilled product. At any point, rectifiers could transform it into something unrecognizable or, worse, toxic. From distilleries, whiskey shipped in barrels, permitting any manner of adulteration. In 1870, Brown adopted the new, machine-made, glass bottle, sealed and shipped from his facility, a personal guarantee of purity and confidence for physicians who prescribed it. He and E. H. Taylor later advocated for the Bottled in Bond Act, further guaranteeing whiskey's quality.

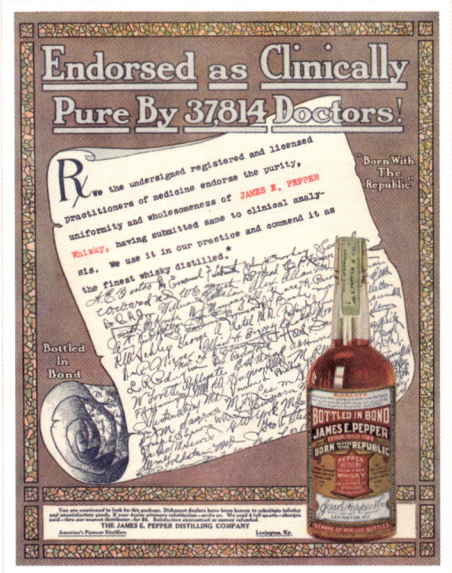

The 20th century further defined the purity of whiskey as medicine. The Pure Food and Drug Act of 1906 delineated the criteria of its manufacture and maturation. Many of those regulations remain in place. The jaws of Prohibition, which still bite us today, also defined whiskey's purity—but not in the way you might expect.

In 1916, the Bureau of Chemistry (predecessor to the FDA) removed whiskey and brandy as medicinal standards, but at Prohibition, they went back on the table. The Volstead Act prohibited the "manufacture, sale, and transportation" of alcohol, but it made allowances for medicinal whiskey, *spiritus frumenti* ("spirit of grain"). The federal government created permits for this medicinal whiskey, which it granted to six distilleries: American Medicinal Spirits, Brown-Forman, Frankfort, Schenley, Stitzel, and Thompson (also known as Glenmore). To control whiskey abandoned or forgotten in warehouses all over the country, the government passed the Concentration Act in 1922, consolidating all maturing barrels, which contained approximately 25 million gallons of whiskey, into 30 warehouses, making it easier to track them. Only distilleries with concentration warehouses could continue distilling for medicinal purposes and only to maintain supply.

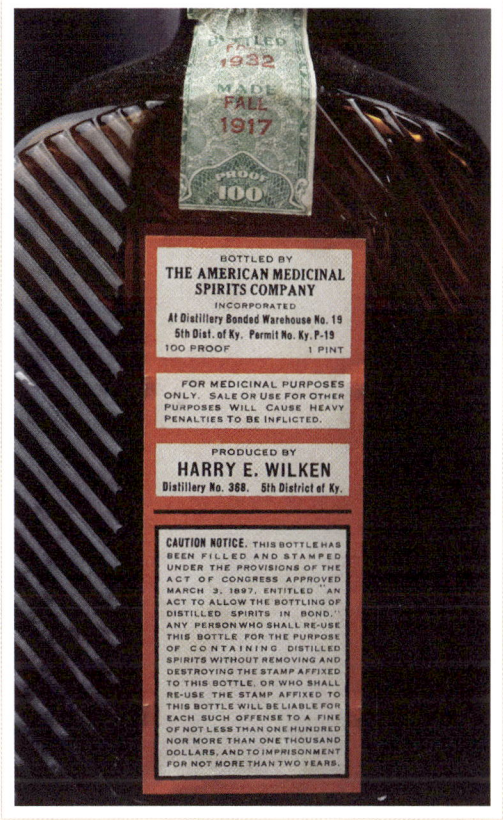

Kentucky producers had a few years to prepare for the inevitable shutdown and ramped up production prior to the act going into effect. The unintended consequence was that some of the oldest whiskey in America was being packaged into pint-size medicinal bottles. This practice harkened back to the medicines of an earlier generation. In an ad from the early 1900s, James E. Pepper professed that more than "30,000 physicians have tested, prescribed and dispensed" their bourbon "in their clinical work." If today you're inundated by drug ads on TV, you've found their source, minus the catchy jingles.

BOURBON POMPEII

MODERN DISTILLERIES ARE A TRIUMPH OF PLUMBING. FROM MASH tuns to fermenters, they hold sometimes thousands of gallons of liquid in single vessels. Fat copper pots and gigantic, sequoia-like metal columns connect to one another in a maze of pipes, valves, and pumps that a distiller dutifully tends to keep the flow moving.

One definition of *plumb* means "level," and a plumber makes sure that liquid travels as efficiently and rapidly as possible from one point to another with no interruptions. For the most part, gravity pulls the liquid. In the days before the steam engine became standard distilling equipment, distillers relied on gravity to get the grain to the glass in as few steps as possible with the greatest ease.

In 1870, Edmund Haynes Taylor Jr. bought the Frankfort, Kentucky, operation founded by Hancock Lee in the late 1780s, naming it OFC (Old Fired Copper or Old Fashioned Copper). It still inspires amazement and wonder. Taylor wanted to create the first modern distillery. He had a series of mash pits and fermenting vats dug deep into the ground, lined with cement, and clad in copper. His unsung achievement, they carried the grist to the mash pits to create the wort, which pumped to an adjacent pit, also lined copper, where yeast entered the mix and fermentation took place. Each of the eight vats could hold more than 14,000 gallons of fermented beer, which flowed to a beer well, where it waited to be pumped into the beer still for its first pass into whiskey. Taylor knew the importance of copper and made sure that the liquid touched nothing else during its trip. The whole operation used only one pump, and gravity did the rest.

The brilliance of the design was almost never known. The plant survived fires and Prohibition and passed through a Ferris wheel of ownership, from George T. Stagg to Walter Duffy to Albert

Blanton to Schenley to a private investor group. Finally, Sazerac purchased it in 1992 and changed the name to its current Buffalo Trace.

In 2016, Buffalo Trace, focused on the nascent "bourbon tourism" revival, decided to convert a large storage building to an event space and uncovered a surprise: fermentation pits, channels, and raceways covered in cement. Underneath lay the remnants, nicknamed Bourbon Pompeii, of what may be the oldest, most intact distillery in America. After careful excavation worthy of an Egyptian tomb, Buffalo Trace relined one of the vats in copper and now uses it to ferment the mash for their version of Taylor's 150-year-old bourbon recipe.

E. H. Taylor's list of accomplishments fills a large chapter in the history of bourbon whiskey in America. This last discovery became his crowning achievement in bringing whiskey from the farm to the masses.

WHISKEY AS BIG BUSINESS

Act I

WE COULD SPEW OUT A LIST OF DATES, BUT VISUALS MAKE IT MUCH MORE fun to track the complex journey of a bourbon company, in this first act, Stitzel-Weller.

1850
William LaRue Weller and his brothers sourced whiskey from local Kentucky distilleries and rectified it.

1857
Arthur Phillip Stitzel emigrated from Germany to Louisville.

1872
Stitzel Brothers started a bourbon distillery, selling the Old Fortuna and Glencoe brands. Isaac Bernheim, brother Bernard Bernheim, and silent partner Elbridge Palmer founded Bernheim Brothers in Paducah, Kentucky.

1887
The Weller company became W. L. Weller & Sons.

1893
Weller hired Julian "Pappy" Van Winkle to head sales.

1920
The federal government granted Stitzel a medicinal license to make whiskey during Prohibition.

1903
The A. P. Stitzel Distillery opened, serving as the main source of Weller products.

1908
Van Winkle and Alex Farnsley bought Weller & Sons.

1933

After Repeal, Stitzel and Weller merged to form Stitzel-Weller, which bought the Old Fitzgerald brand from Old Judge Distillery. Stitzel-Weller introduced wheat (instead of rye) into the mash bill of Old Fitzgerald, which became their flagship brand.

1935

Frankfort Distillers, makers of Four Roses Bourbon, bought the original Stitzel facility

1940s

Charlie Farnsley created the Rebel Yell brand, and Old Elk joined the fold. Alex Farnsley and Arthur Stitzel died. Van Winkle took the reins of the company, which eventually passed to his son.

1972

Shareholders forced Julian Van Winkle Jr., head of the company, to sell. Norton-Simon bought it, renaming it the Old Fitzgerald Distillery and organizing it, along with the Bernheim Distillery, within their Somerset Imports division. Julian Van Winkle Jr. revived his family's pre-Prohibition Old Rip Van Winkle brand, sourcing it from Norton-Simon whiskeys.

1984

DCL (Distillers Company Ltd.) bought Somerset Imports.

1986

Guinness purchased DCL and created United Distillers, which still contained Old Fitzgerald and Bernheim.

1992

United Distillers shut down the Old Fitzgerald Distillery, moving production to Bernheim.

1997

Guinness merged with Grand Metropolitan to form Diageo.

1999

Diageo sold the Bernheim, Cabin Still, Old Fitzgerald, and Rebell Yell brands to Heaven Hill and the W. L. Weller brand to Sazerac.

2014

Diageo reopened the Stitzel-Weller facility as the Bulleit Experience.

Act II

NOT TO BE OUTDONE, THE SCOTS PRACTICALLY DEFINED THE WORD *labyrinth* with a corporate creation that still exists in the form of today's Diageo.

1877
Distillers Company Ltd. (DCL) formed from multiple distilleries and bottlers that dominated the Scotch whisky market.

1889
Arthur Bell & Sons formed, which later captured 35 percent of the domestic whisky market.

1972
Hospitality firm Grand Metropolitan acquired IDV.

1962
Gilbey's and Justerini & Brooks (J&B) merged to form International Distillers and Vintners (IDV).

1985
In a hostile takeover, Guinness acquired DCL and Arthur Bell & Sons, later renaming the acquisition United Distillers (UD).

1987
UD acquired the Bernheim Distillery and Stitzel-Weller Distillery in America.

1988
UD launched the Classic Malts, the first time a selection of single malt whiskies is marketed to the world as five regions of Scotland: Oban, Lagavulin, Talisker, Cragganmore, Dalwhinnie, Glenkinchie.

1997
Grand Metropolitan and Guinness merged to form holding company GrandMetGuinness (GMG).

1998
The IDV and UD divisions merged to form United Distillers and Vintners (UDV) as a separate spirits division.

2000
The newly merged company changed its name to Diageo, *dia* for business done daily and *geo* for around the world.

2001
Diageo's name changed briefly to Guinness United Distillers and Vintners Scotland.

2002
The name changed (back) to Diageo Scotland.

Victorian Era

MACHINE AGE

SEAGRAM'S CHARMED LIFE

THE STORY OF CANADIAN WHISKY FOCUSES ON FIVE MEN AND THEIR competitive successes, all within a similar timeframe. The Wiser, Walker, Gooderham, Corby, and Seagram dynasties all crisscrossed and competed with one another. Their combined economic force provided Canada's tax base and allayed tax enforcement on ordinary Canadians until right before World War I. Their combined impact carried the weight of "whisky Canadien" well into our century. None of them had such quirky good fortune as Joseph Seagram.

Of the five whisky barons, only Seagram was born in Canada (into a family that hailed from England). After graduation, he first worked as a bookkeeper but lost that job after getting into a fistfight with his mentor. Consider it one of the luckiest punches ever thrown. After some drifting, he landed in a milling operation, overseeing the interests of one of the investors. The position came with lodging in his factor's home, where he met his future wife, the man's niece. Good fortune was starting to gather.

In most grain mills, distilling happens as a side operation, and in 1868, Seagram saw that line as the future. The American Civil War left the American whiskey industry in disarray, creating an opportunity. Seagram bought out his sponsor's share, and within a few years, bought out another partner. In 1881, the company came under his sole control, and he changed the name to Joseph Seagram Flour Mill and Distillery Company. In 1888, he sold the flour mill so he could concentrate on distilling and blending. An equal emphasis on Canadian sales and exporting to America and Britain propelled him to the front of the pack.

His lasting influence on whisky comes from the blends that he created. His first success, Seagram's 83, still sold today, matures exclusively in ex-sherry casks. In the 1900s, his sons Edward and Thomas took a more active role in the business, putting their own imprint on products, one of which left a long-tail impact. To celebrate Thomas's wedding in 1913, the elder Seagram put together a blend not brought out of bond until 1917, during the Great War. Seagram's VO (Very Old or Very Own) still serves as a back-bar mainstay of saloons across Canada and America. Joseph Seagram died in 1919, but VO later served as inspiration for the greatest brand to come from the Seagram empire. Ironically none of the family was responsible for it, though. In 1928, in the depths of American Prohibition, Edward Seagram sold the family business to Sam Bronfman's Distillers Corporation. Bronfman doubled down on the company's blending protocols, creating Crown Royal, the best-selling Canadian whisky in the world. It turns out that Joseph Seagram's good fortune outlasted his time on earth.

THE WHISKEY TRUST

CRISSCROSSED BY A NAVIGABLE RIVER AND EAST-WEST RAIL LINES, Peoria, Illinois, once reigned as America's most important whiskey city. Germans and the Irish settled it, bringing manufacturing and, with brewers and distillers in their number, a ready supply of spent mash to feed cattle. It stood on the edge of oak, hickory, and chinkapin forests that made it ideal for barrel production, and corn-choked surrounding fields. Into this boom town strode Joseph Greenhut, one of the most powerful figures in the 19th-century whiskey industry.

Greenhut's empire began with the Great Western Distillery in 1881. From this facility, he parlayed the greatest scheme that the industry ever saw: the Whiskey Trust. On both sides of the Atlantic, trusts were becoming a widespread way to increase profits by controlling supply. The Haigs and other members of the

Joseph Greenhut

DCL were creating their own price-fixing arrangements in Scotland and consolidation was brewing among Ontario distillers. But Greenhut transformed trusts into a fine art in America, firmly embedding in it the gangster mentality that it still has today. To "encourage" distillers to join the Trust, his persuasion techniques included payouts, no-show jobs, and physical intimidation. He convinced the brilliant Jokichi Takamine to immigrate from Japan to conduct fermentation experiments with him—until rival maltsters and brewers burned down the chemist's laboratory. In all, Greenhut assembled 65 distilleries and more than 70 industrial alcohol plants into the Trust (called National Distillers now), before the Sherman Antitrust Act of 1890 brought it all tumbling down.

Greenhut died in 1918, but like a cat, whiskey has more than one life. In 1933, Hiram Walker purchased Great Western Distillery and expanded it, making it the

world's largest facility. With the acquisition, the Canadian company now occupied the heart of its supply chain, and so it ramped up production on bourbon, including Ten High Sour Mash, and rye, including its world-famous Canadian Club.

One brand produced there honored all the laborers and factory workers (including my dad) who ended their shifts with a shot of Imperial Whiskey chased by a cold beer. In the patois of a Pittsburgh steel plant, that boilermaker consisted of an "Imp 'n' Arn," meaning the local Iron City beer. In the 1980s, Walker shut the plant and sold the Imperial brand to Sazerac, which moved production to Bardstown, Kentucky. From there, Imperial re-emerged as an "American blend," meaning 30 percent straight whiskeys and 70 percent grain neutral spirits. Trust that Greenhut would have spat on the ground to hear that.

SALADIN BOX

INTERIM TECHNOLOGIES MOVE AN INDUSTRY FROM ONE PHASE TO another, quickly becoming obsolete, whether it is ISDN in telecom or Betamax in video. The malting process, a critical step in brewing and distillation, turns starch in grain into sugar that yeast consumes to create alcohol. For centuries, people spread wet barley on the floor, turned it, shoveled it, and kilned it, all by hand. As distilleries grew from farm craft to big business, manual floor malting became increasingly inefficient. The motion proved so hard on workers' bodies that many of them developed a repetitive strain injury called monkey shoulder.

In the 1880s, Charles Saladin, a French engineer, brought years of malting innovations together in his eponymous box: a rectangular container or trench dug deep into the ground. Above it, a mechanical bridge holds a series of turning screws that reach the bottom of the box. Fill the box with moist barley and turn on the screws. The bridge travels the length of the box, the screws turning and pulling the barley from bottom to top in constant rotation. A brilliant solution to a difficult problem. It was almost immediately replaced with the drum malting

Machine Age

process, which, in a sealed environment, rotates the green malt to control matting, temperature, humidity, and airflow more effectively until kilning. For the most part, distilleries have forsaken malting on-site and outsource that step to large malting houses, save a few such as Balvenie, Copper Fox, Laphroaig, Leopold Bros., and Springbank. Tamdhu is the only distillery with a working Saladin box.

Denmark of all places revived the old Saladin process with a new twist. In 2005, a group of whisky friends opened Stauning Distillery, which makes malted rye and barley whiskies. Their floor process takes inspiration from Saladin but critically combines the steeping process, as well. Instead of using a trench box, they set two long, parallel concrete walls on a concrete floor, bridged by the malt turning machine holding mechanical arms. They spray the barley with water at the same time, eliminating the steeping process to arouse the barley's enzymes and combining two processes into one. The craftsmanship of floor malting meets the technology of efficiency. Their Stauning Floor Malted Rye, with a dose of floor-malted barley in the mash bill, perfectly showcases how to jump 150 years into the future while pulling history behind you.

ASHLEY'S BOTTLE MACHINE

IN THE 1880S, A SERIES OF PATENTS IN BRITAIN AND AMERICA SET IN motion the means to view milk, baking soda, and, yes, whiskey as consumer products delivered directly for individual consumption while maintaining the purity of the contents. In 1882, patents for an automated machine to make glass bottles started to appear. Four years later, the H. M. Ashley or "Johnny Bull" machine created the perfect glass container for whiskey: the small-mouth bottle that we use today.

To understand this disruption, consider this 1887 quote from *The Leeds Mercury:*

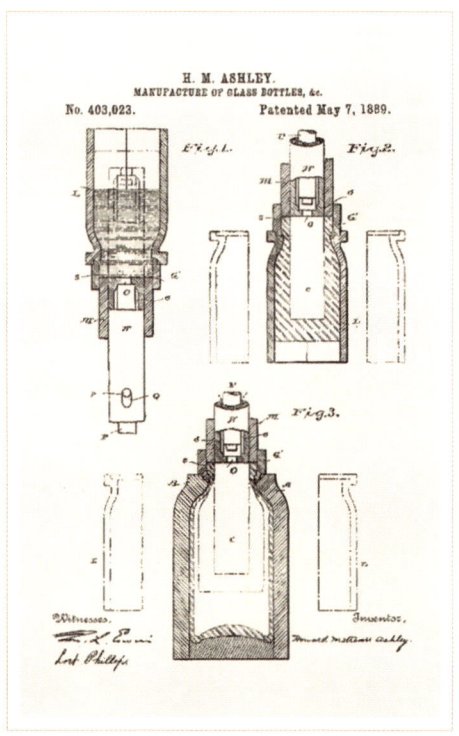

Another familiar land-mark is going. The Glass Bottle Trade is in process of being melted down into new parisons without Blow pipes and Blowers, and instead of 5 men being necessary to evolve an imperial receptacle for beer or aerated water it almost looks as if 5 innocently occupied adults might discover pastime in watching the conjoint labours of a machine and a youth in placing bottles at the service of good liquor as fast as they can be counted. Never since the days of the Pharaohs has anything so clever in glass-making been devised, nor anything so simple. It has remained for a Yorkshireman, Mr. H. M. Ashley, of Ferrybridge, to revolutionize the trade.

Ashley's invention had a historic impact on whiskey. With the introduction of inexpensively made bottles, sherry transport casks from Spain began to disappear,

Machine Age

replaced over the years with barrels that held the fortified wine for a shorter period. With no need to endure the ruggedness of transport, the staves became thinner, which lessened the secondary effect of sherry on the whisky.

Doctors and pharmacists were prescribing whiskey and other spirits as a cure for chills, dropsy, dyspepsia, fever, neuralgia, and more. Since 1870, George Brown, a pharmaceutical salesman and founder of today's Brown-Forman, had been selling his Old Forester Bourbon in handmade bottles as a tangible symbol of its medical purity and reliability. A sanitary, individual bottle of Old Forester was just what the doctor ordered.

But the move to glass proved especially detrimental in Ireland, where the popularity of the new containers contributed to that category's near demise in the 1900s. Dublin distillers stubbornly refused to use bottles, insisting on shipping barrels to points of sale in taverns and inns around the world. As a result, the purity of their product suffered, and the influence of their brands stopped at the bar rather than carrying into the home. Only the Powers Distillery—founded by James Power, a tavern owner—made the switch to glass. But it was too little, too late.

In Scotland, by contrast, Tommy Dewar saw each bottle as a billboard to convey his message, as we'll see next.

DEWAR'S LABELS

TOMMY DEWAR WAS A MARKETING GENIUS. IF HE WERE ALIVE TODAY, he would be a social media influencer with 75 million followers and would be heading up TED Talks on YouTube. Tommy Dewar understood the power of the image like no one before him. He was the greatest whiskey salesman of all time. You can disagree, but you'd be wrong.

John Dewar, his father, a grocer and blender, founded the family business. In 1846, John opened his first shop in Perth, north of Edinburgh. To buy Dewar's blend, drinkers brought their own vessels to the store—jug, decanter, firkin, or similar—and spirited it home. When he shipped it, like all goods of that age, it went by cask to the tavern, hotel, or inn that dispensed it. That all came to an end in 1886 when John passed the business to his sons John Alexander and Thomas. John Alexander took over their father's duties as the heart of the blending operation. Thomas's gift lay in spreading the word, so he became the salesman.

Tommy Dewar

Tommy Dewar realized that shipping by cask was getting their brand name nowhere. The cask head, with their name on it, sat behind the bar. He recognized, one of the first to do so, that shipping in bottles not only guaranteed purity but also turned each one into a billboard. He also appreciated the appeal of provenance. The brand imagery he created lasted for decades: the Scotsman in full regalia. In 1898, in New York City, he created a wonderfully manic short film of four drunken Scotsmen in Highland kilts, dancing under a Dewar's banner. From the top of a building downtown, he projected it for all to see. Later in London,

Machine Age

he created a billboard of a Scotsman, illuminated at night, whose hand appeared to be lifting a glass of Dewar's.

He made a two-year trek around the world, commemorating it all in a book: *A Ramble Round the Globe*. He established the family brand and sales agents to sell it in more than 30 countries, making Dewar's one of the first true global brands. He even weaponized his own wit with pearls of wisdom called "Dewarisms" that fell from his mouth as he drank highballs in London and Paris:

> *"Sometimes doing nothing is doing something."*
>
> *"Minds are like parachutes. They function only when they're open."*
>
> *"Of two evils, choose the more interesting."*

And the one that will mark Tommy Dewar for the ages as the GOAT:

> *"Keep advertising, and advertising will keep you."*

TAYLOR VERSUS STAGG

SCANDAL SHEETS AND TABLOIDS HAVE A LONG, SALACIOUS HISTORY of feeding a seemingly insatiable need to dish dirt on just about anyone in the public eye. So it's a shame that, in the 1870s, a gumshoe reporter or paparazzo wasn't following the tale of George Stagg and E. H. Taylor Jr.'s 13-year battle over trademark infringement.

At the heart of it lies Taylor's signature, which graces today's eponymous bottles of whiskey. Despite the hagiography of Taylor as a dignified businessman dressed in Victorian finery, he was kind of a scoundrel. He faced a lawsuit for selling the same barrels of OFC Bourbon to two different buyers, and he left a trail of debt that frequently landed him in bankruptcy court. At one point Stagg—a merchant, broker, and Taylor's largest creditor—bought his debt and took over the OFC Distillery. Stagg gave Taylor a tiny percentage of the equity and leased the facility back to him to continue distilling.

A year later, in 1879, Stagg created the E. H. Taylor Jr. brand at OFC. Soon after, Taylor noticed the fancy autographs that accompanied fine French brandy and suggested to Stagg that he do the same. Stagg agreed, and Taylor added his distinctive, sweeping signature to the barrelheads, which he knew that taverns would display as they dispensed it. New legislation coincidentally stipulated that barrel heads of whiskey feature the maker's brand.

In 1887, after buying several small distilleries in the region, Stagg and Taylor ended their arrangement. Taylor and his sons bought out one of the facilities and started the Old Taylor

Machine Age

Distillery. On the property, now called Castle & Key, he built (you guessed it) a castle. There, he created the Old Taylor brand, adding his distinctive autograph to the barrels and labels, with the addition of "& Sons."

The trademark battle arose because Stagg continued branding his OFC barrels with Taylor's signature. Taylor sued him, starting their ugly legal saga. Suits and countersuits went back and forth for 13 years. Stagg died in the middle of it, and Walter Duffy, a rectifier of cheap whiskey, purchased OFC. Duffy continued using Taylor's signature during the litigation. In the end, Taylor won, and OFC had to remove his autograph from their barrel heads.

If you're looking for the personal reason behind Taylor's advocacy of the Bottled in Bond Act of 1897, it's right here. He wanted it to put his rival out of business. Ironically, the original OFC Distillery, now called Buffalo Trace, distills both Stagg and Taylor brands.

BABY POWER

Near the register, most modern liquor stores line up mini bottles of whiskey and other spirits so that nimble-fingered aficionados don't "accidentally" drop one into their bag or pocket on the way out. Airlines serving liquor during flights use the nip as an easy way to dole out the right amount of Jack Daniel's or Chivas with a can of cola or soda water. Some states and communities in the US either ban them or are considering doing so.

One of the Big Four of Dublin in the 1800s, Powers Distillery led the evolution of understanding how the market worked. At this time, all whiskey in Ireland, America, Scotland, and Canada shipped to pubs by barrel. The 1880s had introduced mass-produced glass bottles, but distilleries adopted them slowly for a number of reasons: a bottling hall added extra cost to production, shipping became more expensive, and the quick motion of automated parts caused more accidents on the bottling line than anywhere else.

None of that deterred James Power, eponymous grandson of the founder, though, who first shipped Irish whiskey in bottles. Doing so guaranteed the purity of the expression when it reached the consumer, and as Tommy Dewar was proving bottle labels offered a new platform for advertising, in Powers's case birthing the now famous Gold Label and diamond P logo still used today. But as the whiskey became more popular, the price exceeded the reach of the people making it. From an expanded space on Dublin's Drury Street, Power introduced the Baby Power, the first commercial nip in a 71 ml version of the original.

In this era, all bottles had a standard wine cork, as did the first of the Babies. But a standard wine corkscrew didn't work with such a small bottle. Powers redesigned the Baby Power to include its own miniature corkscrew, at first attached to the neck and, later, embedded in the cork itself. This innovation allowed a discreet lady to pop one into her bag as needed, and later generations of fraternity brothers and teenagers on a Saturday night cheered that innovation as they popped their passports to adulthood.

CORRY'S HAND-BLOWN BOTTLES

THE BRITISH WHISKEY INDUSTRY GREW LARGELY THROUGH THE efforts of wine merchants in port cities. They blended malts, pot-still whiskey, or poitín and matured those blends in used sherry, port, or rum casks to add flavor. Establishments such as Berry Brothers and W. & A. Gilbey had set up operations in London, Edinburgh, and Dublin, benefiting from the British government's off-license system, introduced in 1860, and reductions in import duties. The distilleries provided the raw material, but merchants, or bonders, provided the finished product, and their names gained stature as purveyors of quality.

Far from Dublin, Kilrush was an active port city in County Clare, on the "Wild Atlantic Way" of the western coast of Ireland. This is where the Shannon Estuary, the longest in the British Isles, found its way to the sea from Limerick. There,

J. J. Corry, a bonder, took advantage of local commerce, trading in tea, tobacco, musical instruments, ammunition, rum, and of course wine and whiskey. At this time, Ireland was enjoying renown for making the "world's whiskey," especially on the Continent, where it replaced the brandy lost as a result of the phylloxera plague of the 1860s. Kilrush was the last stop before the Atlantic Ocean and the first port before Limerick. The region had numerous small distilleries, but Corry most likely was filling his casks from Limerick Distillery, known locally as the Thomand Gate.

However, the Irish Famine had caused great suffering, leaving the rural populace poor and devastated. As in neighboring Scotland, British gentry owned most of the land, and the natives eked out a living as tenant farmers. Corry resourcefully found two markets to supply. On the one hand, he sold Corry's Special Malt whiskey by the glass to locals and sailors off the merchant ships. On the other, he made special house blends for Anglo landowners and merchants, either filling their vessels or supplying his own ceramic jars and hand-blown bottles, each emblazoned with his name. These vessels shipped to most parts of the island, bringing him some renown as a brand.

More than 120 years later, Louise McGuane, a former executive for Pernod Ricard and Diageo, found one of those branded vessels in a shop. The bottle read, "Mature Irish whiskey, bonded & carefully bottled by J. J. Corry. Kilrush Co. Clare." In 2015, McGuane launched a company that released the first modern bonded Irish whiskey: J.J. Corry The Gael, named after a bicycle that Corry built in his shop. Since then, McGuane has curated an extensive library of flavors that Corry himself never would have dreamed, selling her wares in places around the world that he only could have imagined, as he watched the ships head out to the sea.

TAKAMINE AND THE KOJI PROCESS

MALTING GRAIN LIES AT THE HEART OF BEER AND WHISKEY PRODUCtion, allowing the brewer or distiller to access the sugar trapped inside the grain's starchy content. Before the modernization of the industry in the mid-1900s, malting was a laborious task, employing countless maltmen in every country that brewed beer and made whiskey with it.

A man who says he's got something better is going to upset a lot of apple carts. That man was Jokichi Takamine, who brought with him from his native Japan a process almost as old as malting but far more efficient. In use since at least the 300s B.C.E. to make sake, beer, and shochu in Asia, it relied on koji, a type of fungus, to do the same work. Takamine, an accomplished biochemist from a sake

Machine Age

Jokichi Takamine

family, arrived in Peoria, Illinois, center of the Whiskey Trust, in 1891. Formed by Midwestern distilleries to control pricing and prevent losses, the trust took John D. Rockefeller's Standard Oil as its model. It proved quite profitable at first, as distilleries either were persuaded or threatened to join. By the 1890s, it produced 80 percent of the nation's alcohol. Malting stood at the heart of all that whiskey, and therein lies the threat.

Joseph Greenhut, head of the trust, contracted Takamine's enzyme conversion process to increase output and manipulate his collective's stock price. More efficient in its conversion, the koji process produced more sugar and, because it required fewer workers, saved a vast amount of money. Within months, the *Chicago Tribune* heralded this innovation that promised to "make whiskey cheaper." Within two weeks of the *Tribune* article, a fire burned down the Manhattan Distillery in Peoria where the koji experiments were taking place. Rebuilt two years later, the distillery quickly closed again for good, the victim of the Sherman Antitrust Act of 1890, the "trust buster" legislation that broke the back of monopolies nationwide, including Standard Oil. The American whiskey landscape lost Takamine's process, and the maltsters claimed silent victory over the foreign fungus.

But Takamine's achievements didn't end there. In 1901, he isolated epinephrine (medical adrenaline) for the first time, which made him a wealthy man. As part of a Japanese cultural society, he donated 2,100 cherry blossom trees to Washington, DC—yes, *those* trees. We may have lost his original whiskey, but Takamine's gift blooms every spring in the sunshine of America's capital. The 21st century has revived Takamine's koji process, as well. In Fukuoka, Japan, the Shinozaki Brewery and Distillery distills a single-malt whisky in the Takamine style. It uses 100 percent malted barley fermented with a white koji. In America, their releases first became available, with multiple age statements in limited quantity, in 2021. *Kanpai!*

ABOVE: Barley grain inoculated with koji spores. RIGHT: Microscopic closeup of the mold process.

BULLITTS BEHIND YOUR BEST BOURBON

THE SERIES OF LAWS THAT DROVE AMERICAN WHISKEY LOOKS FAIRLY straightforward: the Whiskey Excise Tax of 1791 that sparked the Whiskey Rebellion, the Bottled in Bond Act of 1897, and the Pure Food and Drug Act of 1906. The names of the sponsors of these pieces of legislation come trippingly off the tongue: Hamilton, Taylor, Brown, Taft, and more. All hold pride of place, lodged in corners of whiskey buffs' collections of trivia and arcana about their favorite drink.

But many unknown people formulated the political strategies, pressed them forward, lobbied them through legislative halls, drafted the language, composed the bills, and in many cases convinced the aforementioned leaders to sponsor them.

One family in particular is responsible for four of the most famous words in American whiskey: Kentucky straight bourbon whiskey.

On the far western edge of the Virginia Colony, Alexander Scott Bullitt, a legal scholar, owned Oxmoor Farm. He helped draft the legislation and constitution that split this region from Virginia to create the Commonwealth of Kentucky in 1792. Bullitt served as the first lieutenant governor of the Bluegrass State. After the Kentucky Distillers' Association formed in 1880, Thomas Walker Bullitt, his grandson, became involved with it and with E. H. Taylor Jr. In 1897, T. W. Bullitt drafted An Act to Allow the Bottling of Distilled Spirits in Bond, otherwise known as the Carlisle Act or the Bottled in Bond Act, the first American act that protected consumers and guaranteed the viability of a particular good: whiskey.

The word *bourbon* as a marketing term was

well known and widely used, even if production varied according to the maker. In this era, Western countries were grappling with the word *pure*. William Marshall Bullitt, Thomas Bullitt's son, belonged to the team that drafted the language that became the Pure Food and Drug Act of 1906, which first defined whiskey. More importantly, he influenced President William Taft's landmark decision in 1909 that formally adopted *straight* and *bourbon* and further defined *whiskey* as we know it today. As a result, Taft appointed him to the post of US solicitor general. W. M. Bullitt later drafted a lawsuit against the federal government on behalf of "10 million proof gallons of whiskey" that eventually led to Repeal in 1933.

Throughout this odyssey of legalese, the Bullitt family home-bottled local whiskeys that they kept or gave as gifts. Unlike most whiskey pioneers, they didn't have a farm still. Only in the first days of 1920, a few weeks before Prohibition went into effect, did they formally adopt a label. In honor of the Bullitt family, the new stewards of Oxmoor Farm have created a bourbon sourced from other distilleries, as the Bullitts did. This time, getting the paperwork done proved a cinch.

Machine Age

20TH CENTURY

DUFFY'S CURE AND THE FALL OF PATENT MEDICINES

I N 1310, VITAL DU FOUR LISTED 40 DIFFERENT AILMENTS THAT AYGUE ardente (fire water) distilled by holy men could cure. Called the water of life in Latin, Germanic, and Gaelic languages, it revived the human condition worn down by the harsh realities of living. The world was simpler then, after all. We consisted of four humors that needed constant balancing and replenishment, and the Sun still revolved around the Earth.

Patent medicines got their start in 18th-century England, a slow lab leak from the old monasteries into new apothecaries of the day. Men of science dissolved ancient herbal remedies into high-potency ethanol capable of shocking the human body back into alignment, whether askew from catarrh, cramps, dropsy, the grip, or any number of weaknesses of the flesh. Imported into the Americas, the cures served as panaceas, and along with cider and beer, people consumed them who had few other remedies to try.

In the late 1800s, patent medicines reached their zenith, exposing the snake oil inside. Little to no regulations for them existed, nor patents, just copyrights. Into this milieu stepped Walter Duffy of Rochester, New York. He transformed his family's wholesale and importing business first into a cider mill, then a distillery, refining and rectifying liquor and cider and producing vinegar. Against local competitors Asa Soule and H. H. Warner, he wanted to corner the market to create the elixir that would "cure what ails ya."

As part of his bold, bald-faced plan, Duffy's Pure Malt Whiskey made no attempt

to disguise its not-so-secret ingredient. The whiskey not only would end your suffering, but it also would cure you of indigestion, hemorrhages, consumption, malaria, and even drunkenness. But wait, there's more! It also promised to prevent them from happening again. His ads declared that more than two thousand hospitals used it and more than seven thousand physicians prescribed it. He solicited testimony from clergymen across the country who supported his claims, including avowed temperance supporters cured of the ailments that bedeviled them. Cured, I tell ya!

But karma can be a bitch. Duffy made a play for George Stagg's OFC Distillery in Kentucky and, in doing so, made an enemy of former owner E. H. Taylor Jr., sparking the latter's advocacy of the Bottled in Bond Act of 1897. Then in 1903, *Collier's* magazine ran an 11-part exposé of patent medicines, spurring the passage of the Pure Food and Drug Act of 1906 and driving a stake in the heart of the patent medicine industry.

When I was a child, I heard that older men with stomach ulcers drank Scotch and milk because it was just like "medicine." Even then, Duffy's water of life still had a grip on the grip.

20th Century

HOTALING'S WAREHOUSE

IN 18TH-CENTURY AMERICA, PITTSBURGH, PENNSYLVANIA, AT THE start of the Ohio River, served as the gateway to the West. It witnessed the birth of American whiskey in the form of rye and the rise of the Monongahela style of rye whiskey. As the 1800s rolled in, the frontier moved west to Kentucky, newly partitioned from Virginia and attracting the next wave of pioneers. As the wilderness across the Mississippi beckoned, they turned native corn into whiskey to make bourbon.

Steam-powered paddle boats navigated the Mississippi to meet the newly created transcontinental railways in the marketplaces of Illinois and Missouri. From there, merchants sent their barrels to either coast without long, arduous sea trips. If they were heading west, they followed the gold rush to San Francisco, epicenter of California cultural life then. When they arrived, A. P. Hotaling held open the doors of his new warehouse.

Born in New York State from a Dutch English background, Anson Parsons Hotaling sought his future out west. In 1852, he booked passage around South America—because the Panama Canal didn't exist yet—and landed in San Francisco, the western "capital of sin." Smart and ambitious, he started his own company and, in 1866, built a massive Italianate warehouse to house it. By 1880, he had become the largest liquor wholesaler in the City by the Bay, with annual sales of 1,750 barrels. He died in 1900, but his warehouse has had a life of its own since then.

A. P. HOTALING.

People felt the 1906 San Francisco earthquake as far north as Oregon, south as Los Angeles, and east as central Nevada. It unleashed a massive firestorm that burned for four days and leveled an entire section of the city called Devil's Acre. Inside that section sat Hotaling's warehouse, holding liquor and an enormous trove of luck. To control the blazes, firefighters blew up any building that

stood a chance of spreading the fire. They marked Hotaling's warehouse, next to a government building holding records, for destruction, but firefighters quickly learned what lay inside and how their plan would spell disaster. So, the US Navy dragged a length of hose more than a mile from the bay at Fisherman's Wharf, over Telegraph Hill, to the building. They tapped a sewage line and sprayed a shower of sea water and muck over the building, which—holy crap!—saved it. The building stands today, in the shadow of the Transamerica Pyramid.

In his life, Hotaling didn't have a reputation as a religious man, and he rankled the local temperance movement. Many local clergy saw the earthquake as divine retribution against the sinful city. So there's a special irony that his liquor warehouse survived while dozens of churches were leveled or burned. A local poet of the day, Charles Kellogg Field, had the last word, as you'll see at the end of the plaque below.

20th Century

MARYLAND RYE

IF YOU THINK OF AMERICA AS A LAND OF DISTILLERS, THINK AGAIN. IT was a land of fermenters and rectifiers. Anyone with a tub who could gather fallen fruit could ferment, and rectifying turned the undrinkable into something pleasant. But distilled beverages primarily came from abroad. The Dutch brought genever, and the British and French both had a taste for brandy. The affluent and elite, who settled in coastal cities from Boston to Savannah, consumed it all.

The British and French battled to rule the sugar trade of the Caribbean. Port cities under their influence sprouted sugar-processing plants. Molasses, its by-product, created rumbullion, the predominant distilled beverage of the East Coast. As immigrants pressed inland, away from taxes on molasses, they distilled grain. Germans brought kornschnappes—a rough, rye distillate flavored with herbs—to Canada and the Northeast. But the markets lay on the coast, and distilled rye from New York, Pennsylvania, and Maryland tasted mostly unpalatable to the ruling class. In the busy ports of Philadelphia and Baltimore, it mixed with other spirits, a little kick of rye to goose the rum or brandy, port or applejack. Over time, the ratios reversed, evolving into rye whiskey modified by those ingredients. Others found that rye and corn whiskeys blended nicely. The possibilities were endless. It wasn't about distilling so much as rectifying the result to please consumers in those port cities.

That's how Maryland rye began. It never had its own federal designation because its beginnings were as amorphous as its ingredients. In the 1900s, as purity laws took hold and whiskey became a defined entity, rectifiers eliminated the rum, juices, and brandy. The rye-corn combination came to suggest Maryland rye's past. Labels advertised "pure rye" to carry the distinction further. The federal government defined rye whiskey with a minimum of 51 percent of that grain, but Maryland makers could mash that with 49 percent corn or add 49 percent grain neutral spirits and still obey the law. They never had a formula, rule, or code. Production of rye in the Old Line State peaked in 1911 with 5.6 million gallons of whiskey from 44 distilleries. Brands came and went, and Prohibition and World War II tore apart the industry. Last out the door was Pikesville Rye, which Heaven Hill bought in the 1970s.

Since then, rye whiskey has become an official symbol of Maryland. Sagamore Spirit isn't the first distillery to open in Baltimore in the last 40 years, but they're reinventing the category for a different time and different consumers. Their American Rye Whiskey combines straight rye whiskeys with two mash bills: one low-rye with a corn lead, the other high-rye and no corn, each processed separately before blending. It leaves the faint echo of the days before Prohibition in America's busy ports.

SWEATING BARRELS

ORIGIN STORIES OF WHISKEY BRANDS RUN THE GAMUT FROM DIScovery and rediscovery to accidents, opportunities, and outright stubbornness. But Publicker Industries in Philadelphia stood at the center of its own, strange little empire with an afterlife still dotting the shelves of stores and bars.

In 1913, Harry Publicker got his start by sweating used whiskey barrels with steam and hot water to release the liquid trapped in the wood, which he sold as whiskey. (Swishing barrels entails filling them partially with water and rolling them for weeks.) He even fought the tax collector, claiming the original whiskey maker paid the necessary tax, so he didn't have to. This kind of immigrant moxie perfectly fit the 20th century, and within a few years, Publicker had a distillery on the Delaware River. Coming into World War I, he had converted to industrial alcohol and whiskey, and by the time Prohibition hit, he was making 6 million gallons of alcohol per year—not to mention a fortune from high-nutrient cattle feed from the waste materials.

20th Century

Publicker retired in time for son-in-law Simon "Si" Newman to take over at Repeal. In 1933, Newman opened Continental Distilling Company a few blocks away, and a host of inexpensive blends resulted: Embassy Club, Old Classic, Charter Oak, and the notorious Philadelphia, now playing in a plastic jug on the bottom shelf of your corner liquor store. At the heart of these creations stood Carl Haner, a chemist who had come up with a way to age whiskey artificially. (Years earlier, when Pappy Van Winkle and Alex Farnsley took ownership of the Stitzel-Weller Distillery in 1908, a famous sign posted outside said, "No chemists allowed! . . . This is a distillery, not a whiskey factory." Ironically most master distillers today are trained chemists.) Haner innovated these brands as well as Rittenhouse, now owned by Heaven Hill. By the end of World War II, whiskey stocks had fallen to their lowest point, and Haner's techniques revived the company.

In the 1960s, Newman and Haner created Inver House Scotch Whisky, their peak achievement, named after Newman's Philadelphia mansion. At the time, Americans regarded pretty much all blended Scotch as classy. Green plaid clad the label for whisky blended from the Balmenach, Balblair, Knockdhu, Pulteney, and Speyburn facilities. At one time, Publicker used, owned, and sold these facilities and others.

Publicker's run ended as contentiously as it had begun. Continental Distilling idled in 1982 and eventually turned into an empty lot. In 1987, an explosion killed two workers, and the investigation that followed identified Publicker Industries as one of the world's worst superfund sites. It took 14 years and $20 million to bring it to rest, resulting in a sad but fitting end to Harry Publicker, the king of sweat.

TEACHER'S SELF-OPENING BOTTLE

THERE'S NOTHING LIKE OPENING A NEW BOTTLE OF WHISKEY. GATHER a good friend or two; buff the glassware; admire the label, provenance, cask number, and significance of its heritage; pull the tiny tag at the top to unwrap the foil cap; and . . . you forgot the corkscrew!

That doesn't happen anymore because you just twist the cap to open the bottle. The cork inside the neck attaches to an external rim or knob that sits atop the bottle. In most cases, only a small twist can extract it, and you're ready to go. We have Teacher's Highland Cream Scotch Whisky to thank for that simplicity.

After Ashley's bottle machine allowed for mass-produced bottles, whiskey shipped in the same bottles as wine and also used cork as the closure. Then, as now, wine corks tapered from top to bottom, and drinkers needed a corkscrew or other device to remove it. Depending on the quality, it could crumble or break,

leaving no ability to seal the bottle again. Knocking off an open bottle of Bordeaux in one sitting is one thing. Knocking off a bottle of whiskey is a great way to lose a weekend.

In 1830, William Teacher got his start as a grocer, which he parlayed into Glasgow's biggest chain of dram shops. In 1876, he died, and Agnes, his youngest daughter, married Walter Bergius, who usefully had a background in engineering and analysis. In 1893, William Bergius, their son, joined the firm under the eye of his uncle, Adam Teacher. In 1913, young Bergius invented and received a patent for a self-opening bottle in which the cork tapered from bottom to top, capped with an external rim at the opening. With the widest part of the cork down in the neck, removal was literally a twist. The innovation of Teacher's self-opening bottle helped it against a bevy of competitors, including Dewar's, Usher's and Ballantine's. Teacher kept ahead of the pack for 15 years before the patent expired and others legally could copy the design. Some bottles have a "throw the cork in the fireplace" attitude, but now you have a choice.

HATCH'S NAVY

TODAY'S STRUCTURE OF ONTARIO'S DISTILLERIES RESEMBLES A BYZantine maze of ownership quite different from its 19th-century beginnings. French giant Pernod Ricard owns Corby Wines and Spirits, which in turn owns the Gooderham & Worts, Lot 40, and Wiser's brands. Pernod Ricard also owns the Hiram Walker and Sons Distillery, which distills those brands. Canadian Club is made there as well, but Suntory owns that brand. We can look to Henry Corby, one of Canada's Gilded Age whisky barons, as another case study in how corporate consolidation affects a brand's journey, and we can look at Harry Hatch, an enterprising salesman, to see how it's done.

Corby's journey started predictably enough. An English immigrant, Corby opened a grist mill in Ontario and expanded into distilling. His success allowed him to pass the business to son Harry, who transformed it into a juggernaut, with modernizations and expanded exports into post–Civil War America. In 1905, Harry Corby sold the entire operation to Mortimer Davis, who continued the expansion and success until the Great War era, purchasing J. P. Wiser's distillery in 1918.

Harry Hatch

At that point, war-time alcohol production and America's Volstead Act decided how history would unfold.

With profits down, Davis hired salesman Harry Hatch. Hatch's journey to this point made him the perfect model of alcohol entrepreneurialism. In Ontario wharf towns, he had operated bars and saloons. He owned package stores and even created a mail-order business for liquor. But in 1920, when Prohibition took effect in America, his genius came into play. He and his sister floated loans to local fishermen to expand their operations and upgrade their fleet. When the loans came due, Hatch had a perfect ploy to assist them in their debt payments. He recruited them into what became known as Hatch's Navy. They filled the hulls of their ships with Corby whisky and then sailed across the lakes to "agents" waiting on the US side. But that was only the beginning.

Seeing the effect on sales revenue, Hatch approached Davis for a cut of the profits, in effect an equity partnership. Davis immediately responded "No," violating rule number one of good sales: In flush times, don't tick off your top earner. Hatch left Corby and purchased the ailing Gooderham & Worts distillery, then the ailing Hiram Walker plant. The coup de grace came when Davis, saddled with fines and back taxes, had to sell Corby to Hatch. In one fell swoop, Harry Hatch owned 80 percent of Canada's whisky, making him the largest distiller in the British Empire. Someone needs to start a brand in Harry Hatch's name.

THE MACALLAN 1928: THE WORLD'S RAREST WHISKY?

I **F ONE SUBCATEGORY OF WHISKY HOLDS THE WORLD'S ASPIRATIONS**, it's Scotch—more specifically The Macallan. So in 2023, when a 1928 bottle of The Macallan hit the market with a £300,000 price tag, it was bound to grab attention. Let's try to understand what you'd be getting for the average price of a US home in 2013.

Macallan followed the path of many farm-oriented distilleries of the Scottish Highlands, obtaining a license in 1824 and living through a series of takeovers into the 20th century. Until 2004, their single malt whisky always matured in ex-sherry barrels, and American palates love it sweet. The whisky in question sat in a cask for 50 years before being bottled in 1983. But the owner of that bottle, if ever opened, may be in for some surprises.

As we saw, Ashley's bottle machine led to fewer sherry casks, once the de facto maturation vessel for Scotch. In the early 1900s, drinking sherry fell out of fashion, driving up the costs of empty casks. A few enterprising bonders attempted to solve the problem by sourcing American oak staves. They assembled those casks in Scotland and treated them with paxarette, another fortified Spanish wine made with the must of Pedro Ximénez and Oloroso grapes, two traditional grape varieties for sherry. When used with Scotch, the paxarette treatment approximated the flavors from sherry casks. Regulations today prevent using additional flavoring agents in whisky making, but it's a good bet that at least one of the three casks blended together for this limited release of The Macallan 1928 used paxarette instead of pure sherry.

Next, we have sulfur, a natural by-product of whisky making that shows up in the grain mash. For the most part, contact with copper in the pot still ameliorates it, but The Macallan's stills are like squat pumpkins, with short necks and sharp angles on the lyne arms, meaning that they have a reduced liquid-to-copper ratio. In 1928, distilling technology still used the worm tub as a condenser, nowhere near as efficient as the modern shell and tube condenser. Lastly, sulfur is further transformed by contact with the cask. The long conversation between spirit and wood that occurs during maturation includes an exchange of aromas, an evolution of flavors, and natural oxidation. The best transformations happen in casks that have not been overused, leeched of all their tannins and lignin. Ironically, traces of sulfur make The Macallan appealing, adding a rich undertone of bottom note ripe fruits and a touch of sulfur funk.

The Macallan 1928 is liquid history in a bottle. I would line up like a Soviet housewife in a Stalin-era bread line for a taste. But "rare" doesn't always mean great, no matter how much you pay for it.

SHIROFUDA

JAPANESE WHISKY BEGINS WITH TWO TITANS WITH TWO SEPARATE visions. Shinjiro Torii and Masataka Taketsuru each understood what whisky in Japan should be. The result of their brief collaboration led to the rise of the Japanese whisky industry and their rivalry.

After World War I, Taketsuru—a promising young man from a sake-making family, schooled in biology and chemistry—went to work for Settsu Shuzo, a prominent drinks company. His work there prompted the owners to send him to Scotland to learn how to make whisky and return with that knowledge. During his absence, Japan suffered a recession. On his return, the company's desire to make whisky had evaporated and so did his employment there.

From a family of merchants and importers, Torii had learned the arts of compounding and blending imported wines and whiskies—harsh and inconsistent then—to create products to delight the customers of his import shop. But he desired to make his own whisky to fit the tastes of Japanese consumers: delicate, floral, balanced. Through a series of communications with a Scottish professor of brewing, he learned of a young Japanese man skilled in distilling and blending who had returned from Scotland. A young Torii contacted a young Taketsuru and hired him to help achieve his dream of opening Yamazaki Distillery, where they would create the first true Japanese whisky.

From the beginning, the visions of each man diverged over questions of locale, maturation, and style. But the force of their culture of honor obliged them to continue, compromising when necessary, to complete the task, until they came to a mutual agreement. Taketsuru relented on issues of maturation, and he would have preferred to distill on Hokkaido, the northernmost main island of Japan that was closer to a Scottish ideal. Torii insisted on the area around Kyoto, where a convergence of rivers in a sacred area created a unique environment of coolness and mist. Ever the businessman, Torii also knew that the site lay closer to transportation and trading centers. But Taketsuru prevailed on how the whisky should taste, closer to what he experienced in Scotland. They released that agreement as Shirofuda, "white label," the first whisky made in Japan by Japanese artisans. Japanese consumers didn't view it as a success, however. As a result, the partners split and eventually created rival companies: Suntory and Nikka.

THE FATHER AND MOTHER OF JAPANESE WHISKY

SETTSU SHUZO, A JAPANESE DRINKS COMPANY, SENT THE YOUNG Masataka Taketsuru to Scotland to learn the ways of whisky. Three years of study and apprenticeship at Springbank, Bo'ness, and Hazelburn taught him every aspect of the distiller's art: malting, fermenting, distilling, and maturation. As a boarder at the home of a widow, he met the love of his life, Jessie "Rita" Cowan, the widow's daughter. Their marriage undoubtedly shocked her mother and the staid, Victorian culture of the Lowlands.

After their return to Japan, Taketsuru went to work for Shinjiro Torii, whose company, Kotobukiya, later became Suntory. Together, they created the Yamazaki Distillery. After his contract with Kotobukiya/Suntory ended, Masataka and Rita realized their dreams of making Scottish-style whisky in Japan. They came to Yoichi, a tiny fishing village on Hokkaido in northern Japan, to make his whisky. Here begins Nikka.

The Yoichi distillery served as their workplace, the engine where the brand endured World War II and experienced postwar expansion. It also served as their home, where they lived and entertained. Here, Rita played the piano brought from Scotland while "Massan," smoking his pipe, perused the day's output records.

Rita died in 1961 before he opened Miyagikyo, his malt distillery in a high-altitude area enclosed by mountains. Sandwiched between two rivers and with optimal humidity, it created a softer, milder malt than at Yoichi. Here, he installed his Coffey stills, created in Scotland, in 1969. In 1979, Masataka died at age 85, and he and Rita lie buried together in Yoichi, the "Father and Mother of Japanese Whisky." They had no children together but adopted his nephew Takeshi. After Taketsuru's death, Takeshi took over the company and continued expanding it.

Taketsuru Pure Malt blends single malts from the Yoichi and Miyagikyo distilleries, and it's not afraid of a little peating. It symbolizes the union of this unlikely couple, a marriage of two great souls in one great whisky.

N 1854, WHEN COMMODORE MATTHEW PERRY'S BLACK GUNSHIPS entered Edo Bay, he opened the way forward to introduce Western spirits to the Japanese drinking public: American distilled spirits first, most likely rye and corn whiskey. Eventually British and Dutch traders introduced the pleasures of Scotch whisky, which prompted a few decades of imports. Brands such as Usher's Green Label and Old Parr captured the imagination of Japan's drinking elite. But 75 years passed until the birth of Japanese whisky. Attempts to make it locally—mixing homegrown knowledge of shochu distillation with the "idea" of Scotch—met with little success.

In the first decades of the 1900s, Shinjiro Torii was contemplating this tradition in Torii Shoten, his shop, as he blended and compounded native spirits with imports to create the perfect drink. He wanted to make a whisky with the light, delicate qualities of shochu yet different from the harsh imports he was receiving. He hired Masataka Taketsuru, who had just returned from a three-year apprenticeship in Scotland, to open the Yamazaki Distillery to make just such a Japanese whisky. As we've seen the partnership dissolved when Shirofuda, their first product, failed to catch fire.

After that split, Torii pursued defining Japanese whisky. To the task, he brought a lifetime of blending skills and *monozukuri,* a relentless pursuit of perfection. He also had a secret weapon, the Yamazaki Distillery. Taketsuru had designed the Scottish-style facility, and the operation imitated the Scottish process of malting, milling, mashing, fermenting, and distilling. Suntory, Torii's newly branded company, benefited from it enormously.

Suntory's approach has a notable blending philosophy and distinctive distilling methods, primarily for mashing. They use a closed-top, stainless-steel mash tun and perform lautering, a type of filtering, on the mash. After soaking milled barley in hot water to create a sweet wort, it filters through perforations in the bottom of the tun. This process softens the resulting whisky, lessening malty notes and highlighting fruity esters created during fermentation. Torii took a decade to perfect the system, tweaking it to create a "pure taste, the sensory taste of how taste is made," a process called *bimi.*

In 1934, he released a new Suntory Whisky, which proved popular with the public, reaching the desired balance, fruitiness, and softness. But as the slow fire ignited, consumers called it Kakubin, a reference to the bottle's distinctive square shape. The best-selling whisky in Japan, it's available only domestically.

CROWN ROYAL

AT THE START OF THE 2000S, WHEN THE WHISKEY RENAISSANCE embarked on a whistle-stop tour around the world, Canada seemingly remained at the station. Canadian distillers were battling the stigma of "brown vodka" left over from the 1960s. Consumers assumed that Canadian whiskies were blended with neutral spirits that neutered them into tastelessness.

Except for one brand. It comes in a blue velour sack with golden drawstrings. Your parents had a bottle of it, and so did theirs, which they brought out only for "good" company because its jeweled surface added class to any gathering. Seagram's Crown Royal launched a special approach to making whisky that makes Canada unique in the whisky world. For that, we have Samuel Bronfman and his obsession with quality control to thank. Using only well-aged whiskies to blend, he perfected the protocol of distilling and maturing each grain separately, then blending the results. In the 1900s, his aggressively competitive marketing program helped Seagram's dominate the spirits industry worldwide. When you raise a glass of Redemption Rye, Four Roses, Bulleit Bourbon, or Chivas, you have Sam Bronfman to thank.

Born in 1889, in what's now Moldova, he and his family emigrated to Canada. Eyeing the whisky industry, he dismantled the Kentucky Greenbrier Distillery and had it shipped to Montreal, where he did his first experiments. Then he struck a deal with the heirs of the Seagram fortune. In the middle of American Prohibition, that family lost their desire to keep producing whisky. His takeover of the brand launched Seagram's and Canadian whisky to 20th-century dominance. During American Prohibition, his business prowess triggered intense competition with Harry Hatch, who owned Hiram Walker and Gooderham & Worts. After Repeal, Bronfman and Lewis Rosenstiel of Schenley battled it out to become king of bourbon. In their day, those competitions drove the popularity of each category.

In 1939, Seagram's blended Crown Royal

Sam Bronfman

King George VI and Queen Elizabeth visiting Canada in 1939.

to honor the visit of King George VI and Queen Elizabeth II to Canada, the first time that a reigning British monarch had come to North America. The company made six hundred versions of the blend, some with whiskies more than 30 years old, before Bronfman approved. Today, owned by Diageo, it ranks as one of the top-five selling whiskies in the USA. The blending lab that oversees production has a massive library of every bottling and Crown Royal utilizes one of the few Coffey stills in production today. My bottles of Crown Royal 1959 and 2015 exhibit a flavor DNA that ties them together while still highlighting the advancements in grain sourcing and production over 60 years. That's remarkable. Other whiskies may have more sparkle, flashier marketing, or better influencer appeal, but they don't have the durability of quality established by Sam Bronfman, the king of Canadian whisky.

SMIRNOFF'S WHITE "WHISKEY"

FROM THE 1960S THROUGH THE 1980S, WHISKEY SANK TO ITS NADIR as it went up against lighter spirits and wine. A rough-hewn Marshall Dillon tried to face the cowboy dandies on Main Street and ended up face down in the dirt. Whiskey had seen the drinking public through Prohibition, two world wars, and a global depression. But as an old man's drink, it was on the outs in America, Canada, Japan, Scotland, everywhere. Who wanted to drink with their old man? "Not me!" cried young baby boomers.

In America, overproduction dropped the price, spiraling the product down to the bottom shelf and rotgut status. Wine also played a part. Easy-to-drink wine coolers, such as Bartles & Jaymes and Seagram's Suncoast, tasted light and fruity and came in the same small bottles as Coke and Pepsi. Processed wines—Blue Nun, Mateus, Riunite—allowed drinkers to imagine that they were drinking in exotic locales while quaffing liquid sugar. In 1976, the Judgment of Paris (the Paris Wine Tasting of 1976, a wine competition) revealed that California winemakers had reached a par with vaunted Bordeaux and Burgundy vintners. The hunt for Pinot Noir and even Merlot began with a vengeance. Add gin and cheap tequila, and whiskey was getting gobsmacked out of the highball glass.

Pyotr Smirnov

The worst perpetrator, however, was Darth Vodka, specifically Smirnoff. Clear, astringent, and antiseptic, vodka offered a sad replacement for the rich complexity of wood-aged whiskey, but what it lacked in flavor, it made up in perseverance. Born in Tsarist Russia, Smirnoff was purchased by Heublein, Inc., a Connecticut importer, in 1939. A classic manufacturer's mix-up accidentally screwed whiskey caps onto the vodka bottles of Smirnoff's first run, and Heublein went to market without batting an eye. "Smirnoff White Whiskey—No Smell, No Taste" read the banner that hit the consumer market.

At the end of World War II, the Moscow Mule appeared at classic drink joints around the country, impressing bartenders and customers. (Mamie Taylor, its Scotch antecedent, came 50 years earlier, but that's another story.) James Bond's vodka martinis popularized vodka further as drinkers embraced Bloody Marys, Screwdrivers, and even a Bullshot—vodka with warm beef broth.

Before long, one of the most brilliant marketing campaigns in alcohol history launched: "Smirnoff, it leaves you breathless." Now, the three-drink lunch or a raucous night out supposedly left no telltale trace of booze on your breath as you made your way back to the office or home to the family. The new drinking lifestyle felt fresh, light, and fun. Dark, heavy, and contemplative, whiskey felt like none of those. Thank goodness those qualities have become cool again.

RISE OF INDIAN WHISKY

F ROM ITS EARLIEST FORMS, WHISKEY HAS HAD ASSOCIATIONS WITH healing and vitality: the water of life, country medicine, doctors' prescriptions, medicinal licenses, and so on. So it should come as no surprise that pharmacology planted the seed for the rise of India's premiere maker of single-malt whisky in the 21st century.

Like gin, whisky came to the Indian subcontinent with British colonists and civil servants in the 1800s. The irony? Hindustan, as it was known then, served as an epicenter of ancient alchemy in the first millennium B.C.E. From present-day

Pakistan to the Gandhara region, people pressed palm juice, cashews, rice, and flowers to make arrack or feni for centuries. Around 1835, colonial-era distilleries opened, but they mirrored the moonshine approach of Western countries, using simple terracotta pots and bamboo retort pipes. In the 1800s and 1900s, the British shared a taste for Scotch whisky with the wider populace, but the local liquor industry didn't take shape until independence.

In 1943, Radico Khaitan was the first commercial facility to make Indian-made foreign liquor (IMFL), bulk imports rectified with a molasses-based neutral spirit and bottled in India. In 1948, a year after independence, Radhakrishna Jagdale started Amrut—Sanskrit for "nectar of the gods" or "elixir of life"—on a different path. A chemist, Jagdale had founded a pharmaceutical company with operations ranging from engineering to beverage production. After India's globalization policies and reforms of 1991, the company focused on distilling for IMFL as well as making brandy, rum, and blended whisky under the leadership of Neelakanta "Neel" Jagdale, his son. However, the success of Royal Stag from British company

International Distillers and Vintners (now Diageo) changed Indian palates to prefer a lighter blended whisky with less malt. Amrut found itself with a surfeit of malt whiskies in its warehouse. Neel and Rakshit Jagdale, his son, saw the next phase of the business: a single-malt whisky to rival Scotland's.

Amrut Single Malt launched in Scotland in 2004, and the company's diverse range of single-malt whiskies not only has garnered international awards and praise but has launched India into the race for which country will become the next global whisky powerhouse. An estimated 30 new distilleries have opened in the country, with major investment coming from Diageo and Pernod Ricard. That spoonful of sugar makes the medicine go down much easier.

COLD WAR

KNAPPOGUE CASTLE

WHEN YOU LOOK AT THE STATE OF WHISKEY TODAY IN THE 21ST century, we are awash in the secondary market of "dusty" bottles—those brands and bottles made in a far-off time that have fired the imaginations, and wallets, of both aficionados and straight-out con men.

There was a time, however, when a whiskey lover bought loads of old stock from a closed distillery, because . . . well, he wanted to drink it. That person was Mark Edwin Andrews, who rolled through an Irish fog into a portal of history.

Andrews was an actual Texas oilman from Houston in the 1960s and a lover of Scotch whisky. He and his wife, Lavonne, a distinguished architect, were touring Ireland in search of an old castle that she would renovate for them to live in, and on the way back to the US, were fogged in at the Shannon Airport. Hiring a driver to tour the area, they discovered a 15th-century castle on the "hill of the kiss," otherwise known as Knappogue. Stripped of all ornamentation and empty, it still retained the regal bones from its initial construction. They bought it, and Lavonne began the arduous process of restoring it to its original splendor.

At this time, Irish whiskey was in its own doldrums. The over two hundred registered distilleries from the start of the 20th century were sadly reduced to four: Bushmills in Antrim, Northern Ireland; Cork Distillers in the south, in Cork; and Powers and Jameson in Dublin. The hundreds of smaller distilleries in the interior had folded, as well. One of them was called Tullamore DEW, which itself was resurrected from an old farm distillery called B. Daly. Andrews found a broker who happened to have a few barrels left: pure pot still whiskey, made of malted and unmalted barley and whatever other grain was available to beat the tax man. It was distilled twice in 1951 and aged in used sherry butts. Over the next five years, Andrews would disgorge some of the honeyed, oily, and lush liquid to be bottled for themselves and for friends to enjoy. Soon, he created a label, found the right bottles, and Knappogue Castle 1951 was born.

Cold War

Enter now their son, Mark Andrews III. As enterprising as his parents, he created a company, Great Spirits, with the idea that others would also love to sip a bit of liquid history. From that came the company now called Castle Brands. Subsequent bottlings of Knappogue Castle were produced at the old Cooley Distillery from 1990–1992 and from there, at Bushmills since 1994, where it slowly morphed into the triple-distilled single malt style it is today.

The 1951 was the first link to what Irish whiskey was like in its glory days. Aficionados knew a good drink when they tasted it, and they pretty much drank it all. You'd be lucky to find a bottle now, and that's the way it should be: *not* gathering dust on someone's shelf.

SHIRAKAWA OF THE GOLDEN AGE

We can segment whisky in Japan into four eras: before discovery, growth years, postwar gold, and global renewal.

Prediscovery began in 1854 with Commodore Perry's gunboats sailing into Edo Bay. His ships carried American whiskeys, and British traders later brought gin and Scotch, the latter of which caught the fancy of the Japanese elite. The Scotch they tasted included Usher's and Dewar's, which, to the Japanese palate, tasted over the top. The Japanese blended those blends further with shochu, sake, tea, juices, and even water.

The partnership between Shinjiro Torii and Masataka Taketsuru began the growth era. Both men worked for drinks companies that produced or imported a variety of products. Both men wanted to make whisky in Japan, and the dissolution of their partnership eventually resulted in the formation of Suntory and Nikka, both of which are whisky powerhouses today.

Daikoku Budoshu, another spirits producer, built the Shirakawa Distillery in 1939, but World War II completely disrupted the industry. The Japanese government compelled distilleries to convert to manufacturing industrial alcohol.

After the war, with an influx of Western soldiers during the Allied occupation, came a golden era. In it, the Japanese drank blends that they altered for consumption. Producers made single malts specifically to blend with grain whiskies to create the dozens of brands on the shelves. In the late 1940s, Takara Shuzo Co. revived Shirakawa, using it to make malt whisky for their popular King Whisky blend. Suntory's "Tory bars" featured their Kakubin whisky as other drinking spots opened throughout the country, featuring whisky highballs called mizuwari. Much like wine and beer in the West, whisky drinking in Japan functioned as a highly social affair and an important accompaniment for food.

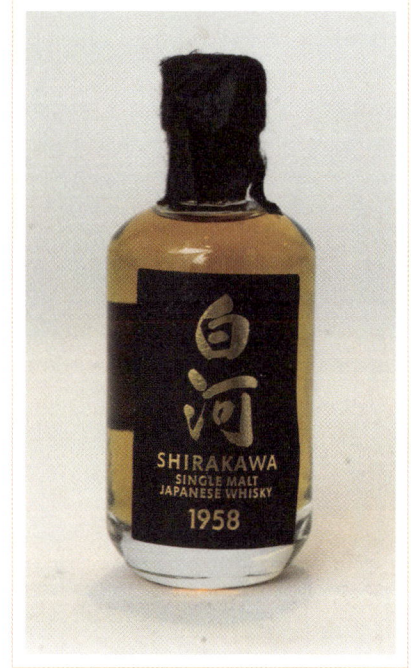

Toward the end of the century, tastes changed, and whisky declined here as in the rest of the world. In the 1970s, Takara Shuzo and other beverage companies shifted to making shochu. Japanese single malts, as a unique product, arrived in the mid-1980s with Suntory's Yamazaki. The Shirakawa facility was demolished in 2003 just as the Western world, first Europe then America, was (re)discovering Japanese whisky, leading to the global renewal of today. Age-statement whiskies, reflecting the age of the youngest whisky in the bottle, from Nikka and Yamazaki now command high prices, and new brands appear almost yearly.

This crazy expensive bottle of Shirakawa single malt was born in 1958, during the heyday, and it's the earliest known single-vintage Japanese whisky. Containing 100 percent malted Japanese barley, it aged in mizunara oak, was transferred to ceramic jars, and then went into stainless steel. Reading history is one thing. This is its liquid equivalent. *Kanpai!*

THE CERAMIC SIZZLE

IN THE EARLY DAYS OF COMMERCIAL WHISKEY, REGARDLESS OF THE country, drinkers went to a grocery store owned by Dewar, Walker, Brown, or the Berry Brothers with their own containers: flask, goatskin, firkin barrel, ceramic urn, or a hand-blown bottle bearing a crest or insignia. Each had its value, whether its ease of transport or its symbolism of personal wealth and taste.

In the 1880s, after the introduction of Ashley's bottle machine, glass bottles became the preferred method of bottling, shipping, and branding. For George Brown, the individual glass bottle guaranteed quality; it offered an advertising billboard for Tommy Dewar's labels; and for Alexander Walker, the square bottle with the offset label packed tightly and shipped easily.

The bottles became easier to open, first with Teacher's "self-opening" bottle, which inverted a wine cork; the brewing industry's press-on, pop-off cap; and in the 1930s, the twist-off cap. Companies recognized the importance of bottle shape and label content for brand identity. Some adopted the dark glass that wine bottles use

for cost efficiency and to prevent UV light from causing spoilage. Each one found its way onto the shelves of stores and bars, and consumers responded in kind.

Then the downturn came, caused not by war or famine but by the changing tastes of the baby boomers. Turning their backs on whiskey, the postwar generation gravitated toward lighter, colorless spirits. In a heartbeat, the whiskey industry fell into the cellar, where it languished for the 1970s, '80s, and most of the '90s. Pressed to the wall, savvy marketers responded with a proven marketing technique: If you can't sell the juice, dress up the container. Behold the ceramic jug.

Everyone got into the act. In Japan, Suntory and Nikka used floral imagery, animals, and classical Japanese art. In America, Stitzel-Weller replicated 19th-century pharmaceutical compounding jars and modern fire trucks. Michter's revived Queen Nefertiti of ancient Egypt, and Jack Daniel's and Brown-Forman replicated the old-timey jugs with finger handles that Grandpa used. Some companies created them as celebrations, such as Jim Beam's for the centenary of the Order of the Elks in 1968 or to showcase the art of noted wildlife artist J. Lockhart. In Canada, Calvert, Hiram Walker, and Seagram opted for elegant decanters of geese and ducks. *Even if they don't like the whiskey, they'll buy it for the decanter, put it on their mantle, and show it off to friends and family,* mused ad execs around the world. And it worked. It got us through the desert, and they still look great above the fireplace.

Cold War

BIRTH OF THE SINGLE MALT

LET'S START WITH A SCANDAL. FROM 1890 TO 1900, MORE THAN 40 new distilleries started in Scotland, producing more than 89 million gallons of whisky in bond. For Tommy Dewar and others, that spike raised a red flag. What was going to happen if they couldn't sell all that whisky? That red flag forecasted an "irrational exuberance" that, in a supply-demand economy, predicates all market crashes. Competing with Dewar were brothers Robert and Walter Pattison, owners of Pattison, Ltd., one of the biggest bottling firms in Scotland. They bravely went up against the DCL (Distillers Company Ltd.) monopoly, gamed the system by inflating profits, caused a whisky crash, and in 1901 spent a few years in jail for fraud.

In an area of the Highlands called Glenfiddich, a young William Grant and his family built one of those 40 new distilleries. In the crash, Grant saw an opportunity to launch his own brand, Grant's Stand Fast Blended Whisky, with the tagline "Always the Same." He knew that blending obeyed the vagaries of supply and demand, which caused the crash, so Grant and his sons built a distribution arm in Europe to ensure their independence.

As we skip into mid-century, Johnnie Walker had hit its stride; Dewar's sat on everyone's bar; and with Cutty Sark, Buchanan's, and Old Parr, the market for blended Scotch whisky had become hypercompetitive. The second generation of Grants, Sandy and Charles Gordon, had a revolutionary idea ahead of its time: *What if we bottled just the malt from Glenfiddich, no grain whisky, and exported it?* It would function as a kind of "pure malt" bottled and guaranteed by the Grant family.

For years, others made and sold this type of whisky locally, but in 1962, the export of Glenfiddich Straight Malt began. Releasing a malt whisky from a single distillery in Scotland kickstarted the conversation about what went into it: the water, the barley, the types of stills, the method of maturation, the people. Suddenly the product had a *story*: kilts, heather, and the geeky details and imagery that every whisky fan cherishes. Over the next few years, Glenfiddich's innovative triangular bottle took on other designations: unblended whisky, pure-malt whisky, and finally single malt. Charles Gordon took off around the world, promoting this unblended malt as far as America and Australia, while his brother Sandy focused on the European market. Dram by dram, bar by bar, bartender by bartender, they aimed to grow single-malt whisky. They nailed it, no scandal here.

THE NADIR OF IRISH WHISKEY

J OHN JAMESON AND SON MADE SUCH GOOD WHISKEYS THAT W. & A. Gilbey, one of their prime agents, kept them for itself to sell. The Gilbey firm had a Dublin office in the Liberties, the city's distilling and brewing center. On one side stood Roe, Powers was on the other, and Guinness lay across the street. But Gilbey so favored Jameson whiskeys that he sent his empty sherry barrels across the Liffey to the Bow Street Distillery to have them filled there and rolled back to his warehouses. After eight years of aging, those barrels produced a complex, sweet elixir with the color of a robin's red breast. An avid birdwatcher, Gilbey chose that name for his brand.

But the Jameson clan and their competitors were running into a host of issues that spelled a collective doom that even Gilbey couldn't fix. They refused to bottle their whiskey, still preferring to ship casks to merchants and taverns, which was costing them market share. Despite using pub spies to ensure quality control, the whiskey was reaching the market severely adulterated. In America, George Brown had proven the confidence factor of sealed bottles for his medicinal Old Forester Bourbon almost a century earlier. After phylloxera wiped out the vineyards of France, and quality brandy production with them, Irish whiskey found favor among the French, but the Scots had seized that mantle. The Irish stuck with their pot stills and the challenging, thick, oily spiciness from their triple-pot-stilled mash, rejecting the Coffey still, invented by one of their own, that had changed tastes to prefer something lighter: blended Scotch and Canadian whisky.

In 1920, the USA went dry for 13 years, and American moonshiners used "Irish" on their labels, hurting the reputation that Dubliners had built. The Irish won independence from the British in 1922, but the British stifled their

A portrait selection of the Jameson dynasty.

trade routes. Roe went under in 1923. In the 1930s, the Anglo-Irish Trade War further strangled trade. World War II, in which Ireland remained neutral, rerouted barley for food instead of whiskey. After the war, export taxes ran high. By the mid-1960s, Irish whiskey had sunk from a high of 80 percent down to 1 percent of world exports.

It took a while for Jameson to learn their lesson. Not until 1966—when the first artificial heart implant took place and the first episode of *Star Trek* aired—did Jameson finally bottle their whiskey in its now iconic green bottle, taken from the colors of the distillery door's leaded glass. But it was too late, the wolf was at the door. It was the same year that, from the ashes of Powers, Jameson, and Cork, the Irish government created Irish Distillers Limited (IDL), which Bushmills joined in 1972, albeit for a brief time. The IDL received investment money in 1988 from French powerhouse Pernod Ricard, which soon buffered declining Canadian distilleries in the same way. The next chapter of the founding families of Irish whiskey and their long struggle leaves them behind as the corporate behemoths shaped the future.

Cold War

THE HIDDEN POWER OF IRISH WHISKEY

WITH THE CREATION OF IRISH DISTILLERS LIMITED (IDL), IRISH whiskey had a chance, if not to revive itself, then at least to stave off certain death. In 1966, a secret conference of the heads of Jameson, Powers, and Cork brought the IDL into being, a rare moment when these fierce competitors joined forces to save not just their companies but the entire industry. The Irish government backed the venture, and all distilling operations in the Republic moved to Middleton, outside Cork, to a brand new, purpose-built distillery. Jameson's Bow Street Distillery and Powers's facility, John's Lane, closed in the 1970s. Arthur Guinness, their anti-whiskey neighbor with the 9,000-year lease, had finally won.

At this point, French conglomerate Pernod Ricard got involved. With fresh capital come new ideas and new ways to look at the marketplace. The pot-still style's time in the sun had set. Drinkers in the evaporating whiskey market no longer had a taste for the old blend of malted and unmalted barley. In 1967, first Powers then Jameson became blends. New column stills, at which Dublin distillers once scoffed, triple-distilled prodigious amounts of grain whiskey along with the pot-still style for blending.

But where to sell it? The last of the Irish distilleries went broke competing for the domestic market as punitive excise taxes sank overseas exports. In the 1980s, a tribe of consultants decided the next move. In 1886, Powers made the move to bottles and at this point produced the most widely consumed whiskey in Ireland. By that metric alone, it should have been a natural for the export market, especially in America. But as

Retired pot still at the old Cork distillery.

consultants do, they considered the cultural implications of the word *power* as a brand identity. The word had enough negative connotations to hold it back, so the nod went to Jameson. Pernod Ricard bought IDL in 1988, and the rest, as they say, is history.

Jameson's Irish whiskey in the signature green bottle has become one of the top five whiskey brands consumed globally. It reintroduced the brand to the world, followed by Powers, Paddy, Tullamore DEW, and a host of others, making Irish whiskey one of the fastest-growing styles in the world.

PAPPY VAN WINKLE'S FAMILY RESERVE

NO HISTORY OF WHISKEY WOULD BE COMPLETE WITHOUT ACKNOWLedging Pappy Van Winkle, but given the estimated 4 million words already written about him and his whiskey, including the family's own book, let's provide just a quick roundup.

In 1893, William Weller hired Julian "Pappy" Van Winkle as a salesman at Weller & Sons, and 15 years later Van Winkle and partner Alex Farnsley bought the company, which made the Old Rip Van Winkle brand. In 1933, after Repeal, Van Winkle and Farnsley merged with Arthur Stitzel to form Stitzel-Weller. Van Winkle became president of the company in 1947. Pappy's son Julian Jr. took over in 1964, but in 1972 shareholders forced him to sell the distillery and its assets to Norton-Simon, a conglomerate. Van Winkle Jr. secured an agreement to retain some of the aged whiskey there, however, and contracted Norton-Simon to produce Old Rip Van Winkle, one of the family's pre-Prohibition brands. At that time, Van Winkle Jr. also started making Pappy Van Winkle Family Reserve Kentucky Straight Bourbon Whiskey. It's a rare wheated bourbon—meaning that, after the corn base, the secondary grain is wheat, rather than the rye of most Kentucky bourbons, making it taste softer and fruitier.

Julian Van Winkle III joined the company in 1981, and three years later released the first Pappy Van Winkle's Family Reserve, combining barrels of different origin, including those saved by his father. By the 1990s, he had acquired enough of the Norton-Simon contract product as well as old stock from another closed distillery and released a series of age-statement Family Reserves, including the first 20-year-old bourbon, the label graced with a picture of his grandfather smoking a cigar. Van Winkle III contracted the Bernheim Distillery (now owned by Heaven Hill) to continue making the whiskey—except no one was drinking old bourbon.

The 21st century arrived with changes all around. The Buffalo Trace Distillery became the new home for the Van Winkle brand, coinciding with a revived interest in practically anything whiskey. Bottles that once attracted no interest suddenly became hot commodities. The whiskey scene started using the word *unicorn* to mean a rare bottle that became untouchable and soon unaffordable. It didn't matter whether you knew about or liked whiskey. Suddenly, at cocktail parties and office gatherings, Pappy's name was dripping from everyone's mouth.

The original barrels held strong until about 2013, when the same formula distilled at Buffalo Trace began replacing them. All are sold as aged for 15, 20, and 23 years. Since its revival, Pappy has driven renewed interest in bourbon nationwide and worldwide because people love to follow unicorns even if they never get a chance to ride them.

LIGHT WHISKEY

IN THE DARK YEARS OF BROWN WATER—AS VODKA, GIN, AND WINE started to replace whiskey—the industry was facing aging stocks, mounting taxes, and intense foreign competition. After World War II, straight bourbon and rye fell out of fashion, capturing only a tiny percentage of drinkers. What whiskey Americans were drinking came from Scotland and Canada, and American whiskey makers struggled to keep up.

Seagram, National, and Schenley, three of North America's biggest liquor makers, each possessed massive factories with giant columns that made whiskey, gin, and vodka. Each was trying to meet or create consumer demand and advertised in magazines of the era. Their operative words: smooth, mild, and mellow.

The Canadian style started with a base of corn whisky, distilled high on the column, toward 190 proof (94.8% ABV), the point at which grain flavor goes neutral into vodka. It blended with separate distillations of malt, wheat, or rye to achieve its light-bodied goal in a hundred different styles. In Scotland, grain whiskies of corn or wheat went through similar processes, high and light, then blended with richer, pot-still malt whiskies. Both styles matured in used cooperage, giving less wood flavor to each. American brands were countering with their own versions—Four Roses, Schenley, Seagram's 7—but the big flavors of the straight whiskeys in them were losing the race. Ironically, the labeling laws to determine the contents and definition of whiskey, for which American companies had lobbied and the 1909 Taft decision had codified, were working against them. In Scotland, the label for Black & White just needed to say "blended Scotch whisky." For Canadian Club, only "a blend" was necessary. Straight was now a dirty word.

Into that state of affairs, light whiskey made its debut in 1972. It wasn't a straight whiskey, nor a vodka. It was both . . . and neither. The distillate consisted almost entirely of corn, high on the column at more than the 160 proof (80% ABV) of straight whiskey. It went into the barrel at 140 proof (70% ABV) as opposed to the 125 proof (62.5% ABV) of straight whiskey. The barrel didn't need to be new or charred, either. All these details produced a lighter whiskey that American consumers were supposed to love. Except the entire style bombed. Most people just ordered vodka on the rocks.

Today, all those barrels of light whiskey aging in warehouses owned by Ross & Squibb (formerly Midwest Grain Products), and others have attracted new interest. Palm Bay International bottles Jacob's Pardon, an 18-year-old light whiskey, at a hair-raising 142 proof (71% ABV) for drinkers who don't want to know the meaning of mellow or mild.

SEAGRAM'S LEGACY

SEAGRAM'S SCOPE AND GLOBAL VISION MADE IT A 20TH-CENTURY powerhouse. In America, it slugged it out with Rosenstiel and Schenley over the massive stocks of bourbon left after Repeal. Under Sam Bronfman and sons Edgar Sr. and Charles, no corner of the world remained safe from their influence. They established themselves in North America, Europe, Asia, and Australia. In Scotland and Spain, they owned distilleries and vineyards. They owned vineyards in Australia and the Willowbank Distillery in New Zealand.

In some cases, they behaved as antagonistic pugilists and take-over specialists; in others, they did straight business transactions. A deal with DCL gave them distribution rights to Scottish brands Haig, Black & White, and Dewars. But their broad diversification across many industries led to their eventual downfall and dissolution. In those end times, their overlap with Kirin Brewing gave rise to a new whisky power while reviving the state of bourbon around the world.

In the 1980s, Europe and Japan ranked as Seagram's largest export markets, with Four Roses being one of their largest brands. In that decade, Japan went crazy

for bourbon, which ironically coincided with the whiskey's downturn in the USA. At the Fuji-Gotemba distillery, which opened in 1973 in the shadow of Mount Fuji, Kirin and Seagram set up a distilling, bottling, and distribution agreement that kept Seagram afloat. But 20 years later, as Seagram was sinking, Kirin purchased the Four Roses brand and its assets, including Seagram's blending facility in Montreal and the Lawrenceburg, Kentucky, plant. Most importantly for the rest of us, the joint venture merged the intellectual capital of Seagram's Jim Rutledge and Kirin's Jota Tanaka.

Both men adhered strictly to the quality control and process orientations of their

The Seagram Building, 375 Park Avenue, the world's first modern skyscraper of glass and steel.

respective companies, combining discipline with innovation. That discipline went further than just manufacturing into marketing, a field in which both companies became acknowledged leaders. Their cross-pollination allowed for the reemergence of Four Roses, with its multiple yeast strains and an eventual leadership position in the bourbon renaissance.

As Four Roses regained its footing and Rutledge moved onto new horizons, Tanaka focused his passions on making a wide array of whiskies: a Scottish-style grain whisky, blends à la Seagram's, and malt whiskies. For years, they sold only domestically, then to Europe and Britain, but today all three styles are available in the American market under the Fuji label. Fuji Single Grain Japanese Whiskey, made from 100 percent corn, tastes light and elegant but rich enough to appeal to bourbon drinkers, which means that it still has a little bit of Seagram's in its genes.

COOLEY'S CHALLENGE

"I WAS BROKE, A STUDENT, OLD AND MARRIED"—HARDLY THE PERFECT conditions to resurrect a dying industry from its own ashes—but John Teeling, descendant of Walter Teeling and doctoral candidate at Harvard, had an inkling of his fate in 1971. A few years earlier, he had witnessed the Irish government help create Irish Distillers to save his native country's whiskey-making heritage. Jameson, Powers, and Cork consolidated, infused with cash to keep operating as they had 80 years prior, when they represented a global powerhouse. They also redrew the rules that defined Irish whiskey's future.

Teeling's dissertation focused on the decimation of the Irish whiskey industry, how it had survived 19th-century temperance movements but fell apart through a sequence of unfortunate events: reluctance to embrace innovations such as the Coffey still and bottling, American Prohibition sinking their biggest market, the loss of trade routes after independence from Britain, and changing tastes that left the prized Dublin pot-still style behind. It all sounded the death knell for Irish whiskey's dominance. After World War II, American consumers believed the mythology that "Irish whiskey gives you headaches." The new rules defining whiskey categories favored the pure pot-still style (malted and unmalted barley) and lighter blends, but it gave short shrift to other historical styles, including single malts and peated whiskeys.

Armed with a business prospectus declaring his intent to resurrect the Irish whiskey industry, Teeling—the older, no longer broke, and still married former student—raised enough capital to purchase an old industrial alcohol factory. The site used potatoes and various grains to make alcohol and occasionally contracted a well-known vodka brand. It possessed the appropriate column stills, and two pot stills from the closed Ben Nevis Distillery in Scotland completed it. In 1987, Cooley Distillery opened its doors, the first independently owned distillery in Ireland in more than 70 years. What he made surprised and delighted a new generation of drinkers.

Kilbeggan, the blended Irish whiskey, tasted elegant and light. Greenore, the single-grain whiskey, came from 100 percent corn and challenged bourbon. Tyrconnell, a rich single-malt whiskey, featured secondary finishes. But the shocker was Connemara, the first peated Irish whiskey to appear in almost a century, challenging the myth that Irish whiskey doesn't taste smoky. These brands led to Cooley's success until 2012, when Beam (now Suntory) bought the operation.

The soul of Cooley lives on in the Teeling family's newest ventures: his sons' purpose-built Teeling Distillery in Dublin and John's own Great Northern Distillery in Dundalk, Co. Louth where his "my kitchen, your recipe" approach to distilling allows for innovation and tradition to flow again.

THE BIRTH OF FRENCH WHISKY

RESEARCHERS BELIEVE THAT WHAT WE NOW CALL BRANDY SHOWED up in Europe in the 1100s, aided and abetted by the monks of the Holy Roman Empire, marking the beginning of aqua vitae. Germanic, Hungarian, and English empires were expanding as the remains of the Byzantine Empire were fading and fighting hordes of invaders from the east. The last of the Arab caliphates, the carriers of the magic of distillation, was still embedded in the Iberian Peninsula, the seat of all knowledge and scholarship. Division was everywhere and Europe was a holy mess.

As the kingdom of France evolved, so too did the alchemy of distilling wine. In the High Middle Ages, eau de vie became popular, especially when made of grapes, from which modern brandy evolved. Through the following centuries, France absorbed grain varieties from its eastern neighbors and in the 1800s and 1900s it served as the breadbasket of Europe. A country of wine drinkers and maker of brandies, France ironically ranks in the top three markets for blended Scotch whisky, so why was no one making whisky here?

Whisky didn't enter the picture in France until the late 1980s, in the middle of a Cognac crisis. The Cognacs of the four large houses weren't selling, but each had a Scotch in its distribution portfolio. Three regions of the country got in on the act: Brittany, the western stronghold of ancient Celtic culture; Charente, the locus of brandy production; and Alsace-Lorraine, between the oak forests of the Vosges and Germany.

In 1900, Léon Warenghem founded his eponymous distillery near the north coast of Brittany, making liqueurs, including Elixir d'Armorique (from Aremorica, the Latin word meaning "place in front of the sea"). In 1987,

Brittany Coast, France

they launched WB Breton whisky, a blend, and in 1998, a single-malt whisky called Amorik, the first in France. In 1995, Edouard Daucourt founded his distillery in Charente, releasing Bastille 1789, another blend, in 2010. Sensing a threat, the powerful Cognac houses wanted to shut him down, and he even encountered resistance from bottlers who didn't want his business for fear of reprisals, but he prevailed. At the Rozelieures Distillery in Alsace, Christophe Dupic, the Grallet-Dupic family's fifth-generation distiller, refocused distillation from Mirabelle plum brandy to single malts of exceptional variety in the early 2000s.

From those three distilleries in the 1980s and '90s, the number of French whisky distilleries has grown to exceed 125, and Whisky Breton has received legal protection as its own, distinct subcategory. What France lacked in whisky history, it's making up in whisky's future.

REBIRTH AT CENTURY'S END

THE NEW AGE OF AMERICAN WHISKEY

THE WHISKEY RENAISSANCE FOLLOWED TWO OTHER TRENDS IN AMERican consumption that by chance originated in California. In 1976, the Judgment of Paris, a blind tasting, marked the international recognition of the United States as a world-class wine producer. Napa's Chateau Montelena wines bested the leading French producers, hands down, surprising everyone—including the Californians.

In the 1990s, interest in home brewing emerged as a counterpoint to mass-market beers such as Budweiser and Coors, unleashing the second trend: the craft beer boom. In San Francisco, Anchor Steam, a beer popular during the Gold Rush era, had come back to life in 1965, slowly starting a brushfire of homebrewers that eventually challenged the giants for market share. A man who understood the corporate mentality so well that he dedicated his entire life to rebuffing it revived the beer. That man was Fritz Maytag, and yes, his family made your grandmother's washer and dryer. After his revival of Anchor Steam, he restlessly eyed the roots of American whiskey: the copper pots of Scotland and the whiskey style of Western Pennsylvania, epicenter of the 1792 Whiskey Rebellion, where, at the gateway to the west, German pioneers popularized rye as a recreational drink. Maytag discovered that those farmer-distillers were using 100 percent malted rye cooked in copper pots.

With distilling partner Bruce Joseph, Maytag began Anchor Distilling in 1994. Two years later, they released a rye-style whiskey that confounded most consumers with an unexpected name, Old Potrero (Spanish for "paddock"). Using 100 percent malted rye and a brewer's yeast, they double-distilled their Old Potrero 18th Century Style Whiskey and aged it for two years in new, toasted oak barrels, as close to the original recipe that current laws would allow. Its deep, earthy chewiness offered a stark contrast to whiskies made on a column. It qualifies as whiskey, though, not specifically rye, because US law requires that rye use a new, *charred* oak barrel. (Toasting applies a lower level of heat for a longer time, whereas charring uses flame contact to carbonize the wood.) That's why Hotaling & Co., which evolved from Anchor Distilling, has added new styles to the Maytag-Joseph collaborations: single-malt straight rye and single-barrel reserve, all under the Old Potrero banner.

If you pick the right target, restlessness has its rewards. Like the beer before it, Old Potrero was setting up a long-term battle between the little guy and the big, bad, nameless corporations that made whiskey. Anchor's version of whiskey history started the tidal wave of craft production in which we're swimming today. If you're going to take on the big boys, it helps if you already know their game.

SINGLE MALTS COME TO AMERICA

SCOTCH WHISKY USED TO BE ALL ABOUT BLENDS, BUT IN THE 1980S, that industry began releasing all-malt distillations rather than selling them wholly in bulk to blending houses. That business move resulted from the dearth of sales in Scottish blends that began in the early 1970s, caused by that generational shift in drinking habits. Brands such as Chivas Brothers, J&B, Cutty Sark, Buchanan's, Dewar's, and Johnnie Walker all watched sales hit their lowest mark since the end of World War II. The lack of orders prompted malt distilleries to take their future into their own hands, and they released their own whiskies, slowly at first. Glenfiddich, The Glenlivet, The Macallan, and even Laphroaig bottles appeared on the shelves of discriminating retailers, and consumers soon learned that "single" meant the single distillery listed on the label; "malt" meant

the whisky came from 100 percent barley; "Scotch whisky" had broadened to mean any whisky from Scotland, not just their favorite blends; and everyone got comfortable with the word *glen,* a Celtic word for a valley in hills or mountains.

Single malts were ascending. Japan, a country dedicated to blended whiskies, got into the act early when Suntory's Keizo Saji, the company's president and son of founder Shinjiro Torii, released Japan's first single malt, made in the Yamazaki Distillery, in 1984. When John Teeling started Cooley Distillery in Ireland in 1987 he did so to revive Ireland's history of single malts by creating two of them: Tyrconnell and Connemara. In Canada, Bruce Jardine started Glenora Distillery in Nova Scotia and distilled Glen Breton, North America's first single malt, in 1990. In Brittany, Warenghem caught the single-malt fever in 1998 with Amorik. In 2015, the EU government even established a protected geographical indication for Whisky Breton.

Steve McCarthy of Clear Creek Distillers in Oregon might qualify as the godfather of American single malts. Inspired by French eaux de vie, he started making pear brandy in 1985, a pioneer of the craft movement. A subsequent trip to Ireland convinced him to make the first US single-malt whiskey, inspiration coming from Lagavulin, the heavily peated malt from Islay in Scotland. Sourcing even a small amount of peated barley in Oregon proved nearly impossible, so McCarthy turned to Port Ellen, Lagavulin's maltster on Islay. Specifying his peat level, he single-distilled the barley in Clear Creek's brandy stills in 1993 and barreled it in garryana oak, a species native to the Pacific Northwest.

McCarthy's Single Malt crawled around back shelves for years because no one could conceive of an American single-malt "Scotch" from Oregon. But since its debut, the whiskey has acquired a barrel of awards, and a new trade organization created to promote it became the stewards tasked with convincing the US government to recognize American single malt as an official category—recognition that was achieved in 2024. Move over, Scotland! It's about to get tight as malted barley takes the world stage.

REDISCOVERY OF GRAIN WHISKIES

IN 1906, BRITISH PARLIAMENT PASSED THE LANDMARK SPIRITS ACT, giving column still whisky (using multiple grains) equal status as malt whisky. After that, producers marketed grain whisky for its own use, mostly medicinal. A premier distillery of that era, Cambus, advertised theirs as "a wholesome stimulant" and took pains to proclaim "Cambus is not Pot Still whisky." Aged in Scotland in the same used barrels as malt whisky, blended together we came to know it as "Scotch": Johnnie Walker, Vat 69, Black & White, Dewar's, Buchanan's, Cutty Sark, Teacher's, and the hundred other brands that allowed Scotch whisky to advance its claim.

In the 1970s and '80s, tastes had changed, and orders for blended Scotch whisky dropped, resulting in cost-cutting measures that lessened quality. Distillers pushed the envelope toward that Maginot Line of 94.8% ABV to capitalize on higher yield in massive column stills. They sourced cheaper grains, including wheat, that lacked the rich sweetness of maize. They tilted the ratio of grain and malt, with grain well past the halfway point that marked the original, 19th-century style. Brands dropped their proof to the minimum 40% ABV, colored them with caramel, and chill-filtered them to remove the fatty glaze—and consequently, the flavor—that would have resulted. Worst of all, grain whiskies were maturing in barrels used *four or five* times, so the wood had no character left to impart to the spirit.

In 1998, the newly formed Diageo hired American John Glaser as global marketing director for Johnnie Walker, the start of his career in the Scotch whisky industry. At that time, blends were declining, malts were ascending, and no sane person bottled a grain whisky alone. In the labs of his mentors, blending legends Maureen Robinson and Jim Beveridge, he

Rebirth At Century's End

saw not only the marketing struggles but also where the industry was shooting itself in the foot: over-processing and barrel overuse.

In his London flat, Glaser blended unprocessed grain whiskies, chancing on a revelation. Some of the older grain whiskies tasted sublime to the point of ethereal. Cambus, Caledonian, Carsebridge, and others that had closed, had used corn as their primary grain and aged the liquid in quality used casks. The whisky exhibited flavors and mouthfeel not found in malt whiskies—or whiskies anywhere. If he could get people to taste these, they'd be gobsmacked at the discovery. Thus were born Compass Box Whisky and Hedonism, a vatted grain whisky blending old and newer barrels from multiple distilleries. It caused a small revolution in modern Scotch whisky that underscores practically every brand today.

A TALE OF TALISKER

IN THE LATE 1980S, I CAME UPON A BOTTLE OF 10-YEAR-OLD TALISKER Single Malt Scotch Whisky, and it tasted unlike anything I'd experienced: briny, smoky, and fruity with a hint of oyster shells and peach compote, a powerhouse of flavor. I typed a fan letter to "Mr. Talisker" and sent it to the wholesaler's address on the back label. A reply from Andy MacDonald surprisingly beckoned me to visit the distillery.

A decade later, I convinced my wife and nine-year-old daughter to take our annual vacation on the Isle of Skye, home of Talisker. In the late afternoon, we made our way to the town of Carbost and the distillery, knocking on a side door. In 1999, the internet barely existed. No voluminous books or blogs prepared us for the workings of a distillery. But the passage of time hasn't dimmed the smell that carried us through the door to the base of the massive copper pot stills.

After the tour, I presented MacDonald's letter and inquired whether he still worked there. "Oh, he's our production manager," the guide responded, snatching the letter from my hand as she walked out the door.

A few minutes later, a dapper older man came bouncing into the gift shop. "Which one of you wrote this letter? Who's Mr. Robinson?"

"I am," I replied, with the weak smile of someone about to be sent to the principal's office.

"Well, lad, it's about time. We've been waiting *years* for you to get here!" he laughed.

Our guide's face lit up, and she led us from the gift shop into the warehouse next door. The whisky casks lay racked on their rounded sides so the cool, damp of the environment could draw the alcohol soaked into the wood. All those aromas mingling in the air felt not intoxicating but mind-bending. It seemed almost holy, like we had entered a temple of expectation, the spirits from inside the casks dancing eerily through the air, tempting us.

MacDonald popped the bung on a cask, pulled out a long copper tube (known as a valinch or a thief) stuck it into the bung hole, and poured the contents over our hands, spilling from glass to glass, laughing and talking the entire time. "Don't wipe it off. Rub your hands together and smell," he said, demonstrating how to smell the base aromas of the whisky without the interference of the alcohol.

We laughed and drank, reveling in the experience. My wife smiled, my daughter giggled at the adults while she smelled her whisky hands, and there I knew that whisk(e)y was going to play a role in some part of my life.

Before you die, visit Skye.

THREE-CHAMBER STILL

TODD LEOPOLD IS A SUPER NERD. AS HALF OF LEOPOLD BROTHERS Distillery in Aurora, Colorado, he takes up some of the most obscure reading material, including old mash bill reports from the 1800s. One of those reports contained a footnote to history, a reference to an obscure device once used to distill whiskey but no longer. It started an itch.

The Bottled in Bond Act of 1897 and the Pure Food and Drug Act of 1906 both established what whiskey was and wasn't in America, and tax compliance followed. In 1907, the Internal Revenue Service commissioned C. A. Crampton and L. N. Tolman to survey distilling practices. In one of their reports, Todd Leopold found the bug that caused the itch: the three-chamber still.

Neither a pot still nor Coffey still, the three-chamber still functioned as interim technology, like VHS tapes between silver nitrate film and DVDs or CDs between vinyl and MP3s. It had a steampunk quality to it—lots of pipes and riveted seams and a process that needed a lot of attention—that identified it from the Age of Engineering. Those inefficiencies spelled its doom: The industrial column still rendered it obsolete. But a super nerd such as Leopold understands that it's not just about reviving an old gadget. First you have to find the right grains to go into it.

The Leopold brothers knew that the American alcohol industry had been "breeding the flavor out of the grains." Nerd alert, it comes down to the ratio of starch and oils in the raw grain itself. Before Prohibition, grains had about 65 percent starch in them, and newer breeds contain more than 80 percent. Extending this starch-to-oil ratio increases yield but kills flavor. "It's an oil-extraction device," Todd says of the three-chamber still, meaning that today's grain varieties won't do it justice.

Leopold worked with local farmers to develop Abruzzi rye, an older variety with a lower starch content (62 percent) and a high oil content. Then he approached Vendome Works

Floor malting at Leopold Bros.

in Louisville with a schematic to create a replica of the still, a device not used in more than 50 years. With it, he and his brother, Scott, made their now famous Three-Chamber Rye Whiskey using Abruzzi rye and his own floor-malted barley, which followed the report's ratio of 20 percent of the mash bill.

It tastes oily, earthy, rich, and full-bodied with notes of roses and elderflower and elegant fruit on the palate. Gloriously complex and delicious, it drinks like rye made before Prohibition. You're tasting history—and you can enjoy it without reading one word of a dry, dense government report. Todd Leopold read it so you don't have to. It's what nerds do.

DIGITAL AGE

BRUICHLADDICH DISTILLERY

WARS DISRUPT. IN TIMES OF COMBAT, WHISKEY PRODUCTION SHIFTS to producing industrial alcohol for munitions and military plastics. In every whiskey-making country, both world wars brought whiskey production either to a halt or a slow drip that resumed only at the end of hostilities.

Changing tastes disrupt just as badly. The bigger disaster for whiskey came in the 1970s and '80s, when baby boomers rejected everything that their parents liked or represented, including brown spirits. Plant closures, layoffs, and other consolidations followed this radical shift in drinking habits. In Japan, Canada, America, and elsewhere, brown water was in deep trouble. By the mid-1980s, Scotland had enough whisky sitting in the warehouses to fill a *loch,* (Gaelic for "lake"), hence the phrase "whisky loch." Workhorse distilleries such as Port Ellen, Carsebridge, Dallas Dhu, and Imperial went silent, were destroyed, closed, or mothballed. Around 40 facilities, an estimated 30 percent, shut down.

Built in the late 1880s, Bruichladdich Distillery stood near Port Charlotte on the western edge of Islay in the Scottish Hebrides. Whyte and Mackay, its last owner,

closed it in 1995. But fortune hadn't decided its final fate. One day in 1999, Mark Reynier, a wine negotiant from Edinburgh, showed up at the locked gates. The guardsman shooed him away with a brusque "Fuck off!"—so Reynier bought the place.

Brought up in the wine trade, Reynier saw it as an ideal place to revive what he considered Scotch whisky's real mission: to reflect provenance through grain heritage. With 25 investors, he reopened the gates and brought in Jim McEwan, director of marketing from nearby Bowmore and a native of Islay island, an Ileach, to run the operation. They revived the Victorian-age machinery, and in 2001, they filled this barrel, with Mark's son, Ruari, doing

LEFT: A mash tun in action at the Bruichladdich Distillery.
RIGHT: Reynier, at left, filling the first barrel of Bruichladdich in 2001.

the honors. While their new whisky was aging for a minimum of three years, the old stocks in the warehouse gave them the perfect blender's playground to create the Bruichladdich style. They created so many single-malt variations that insiders joked: "It's Thursday, time for another Bruichladdich release."

In the meantime, McEwan convinced his fellow Ileachs to start growing *bere,* meaning "barley," on the island to realize Reynier's vision. In 2011, the distillery released the 10-year-old Laddie, made exclusively from their newly revived stills: lightly peated, elegant, and fruity. Their other brands, Port Charlotte and Octomore, reflect Islay's penchant for peat and smoke.

Reopening Bruichladdich indicated that the loch was draining and Scotch single malts were the herald of the 21st century. Whisky, in Scotland and around the world was roaring back, just in time for its renaissance.

FIVE STRAINS FOR FOUR ROSES

YEAST, A TYPE OF FUNGUS, IS THE FOUNDATION OF WHISKEY. THE strain of yeast used in fermentation determines much of a whiskey's flavor profile: estery, fruity, vegetal, yeasty, grainy, and so on. After yeast eats the sugar in the grain mash, its output of ethanol contains flavor molecules shaped during distillation and transformed during maturation. For years, traditional distilleries focused on proprietary yeast to maintain consistency from batch to batch. Jim Beam reportedly found his proprietary yeast growing outside his windowsill. Buffalo Trace in Kentucky, for example, uses one yeast strain for everything, from Eagle Rare to Pappy Van Winkle's Family Reserve. The mash bill, distillation protocol, maturation techniques, and blending make up the remaining brand differences.

The more yeast varieties you have, the more diverse your product line, especially important if you're out to build an empire. This was the heart of Seagrams Distillers, under the 20th-century leadership of Sam Bronfman, who foresaw a world of limitless possibilities: vodka, gin, schnapps, and whiskey. With quality yeast and distilling excellence, Seagram gained a foothold across the globe. In the 1930s and '40s, when Bronfman was acquiring defunct Kentucky distilleries, he obtained more than their physical assets and aging inventories. He also got their yeast strains. One of those facilities was the Frankfort Distillery, makers of Four Roses Bourbon.

Following the postwar quest for lighter spirits, the Four Roses Yellow Label blend of straight whiskeys took on neutral spirits by 1947, and sales ran high for a decade or so. But by the 1960s, tastes were changing again, and an even lighter reformulation failed to ignite. In 1972, the brand partnered with Kirin Holdings in Japan, which pulled the product from America

and focused on selling Four Roses Kentucky Straight Bourbon Whiskey in Asian markets only. Sales skyrocketed.

Then the whiskey renaissance hit, and in 2002, after Seagram crashed, Kirin bought Four Roses outright. Using both Japanese and American ingenuity and a shared sense of excellence, Kirin developed five yeast profiles and two different mash bills, one high-rye, for Four Roses releases. In 2004, they released Four Roses Single Barrel and, in 2006, their Small Batch, both for the American market. The results speak for themselves. Four Roses led the pack that brought bourbon back from the brink.

THE EINSTEIN OF WHISKY

MOMENTS CAN DETERMINE HISTORY AS MUCH AS OBJECTS. BUT people live and record history, and as we've seen, whiskey history features a trove of people who've driven it forward. Names such as Bronfman, Brown, Cor, Daniel, Haig, Hatch, Jameson, Taketsuru, and more appear throughout these pages, each affecting the development of our water of life. These names bring us to the present. Add to that list Dr. Jim Swan, who wrote the playbook for the future.

Dr. Swan advised and worked on dozens of projects worldwide. People whispered his nickname, the "Einstein of Whisky," respectfully behind his back. From barley variety and water purity to distilling protocols and wood management, Swan revealed layers of detail and science beneath each of these processes, bringing whiskey making from the anecdotal to the molecular. His work with the Scotch Whisky Research Institute, where he codeveloped the whisky tasting wheel, and later with consulting firm Tatlock & Thomson, still resonates throughout the industry and changed whiskey making forever. In some ways, we can mark whiskey's history as "Before Swan" and "After Swan." He led with passion, backed it up with science, and remained a soft-spoken gentleman who inured himself to everyone he met. It was Swan's way. He married science to art and, like the alchemists of old, turned everything to gold. In 2002, he founded his eponymous consulting company, and his client list of distillery "birthings" is vast and global. Some appear in this book: Penderyn, Amrut, Milk & Honey, and Lindores Abbey, site of the first known reference to Scottish distillation in 1494 and his last project before passing away in 2017.

Kavalan, his most well-known project, shows the brilliance of his thinking. Distillation's evolution started with ingredients and moved sequentially to the processes of fermentation, distillation, and maturation. For Kavalan, Swan had to conquer the oppressive heat and humidity of the region. To do so, he reverse-engineered the entire process. He started with the design of the variable-temperature warehouse and racking system and worked backward, resolving the particulars of distillation, fermentation, and mashing, in that order. That type of out-of-the-box thinking created his legend and turned Kavalan into an award-winning, global whisky.

When released, the three-year-old Kavalan Single Malt Whisky was bursting with tropical fruit flavor. For Swan, it embodied the Kavalan spirit. That and every subsequent product and release carry the spirit of the master himself.

WALES GETS BACK IN THE GAME

EVAN WILLIAMS DISTILLED ON BOTH SIDES OF THE ATLANTIC, BUT THE whiskey world focuses more on Kentucky than his origins in Dale, Wales, a bucolic region hanging like an appendage off the southwest coast into the Celtic Sea. For most of history, that one place remained the lonely reference to whisky in Wales—and maybe with good reason.

Initially a cottage industry, whisky distilling gave farmers another tool to make use of their crops, using up excess grain. Wales, largely mountainous and devoid of large metropolitan centers, possesses a wealth of natural minerals, including copper and coal, that makes it perfect for mining and extraction industries alongside farming. During the Industrial Revolution and beyond, Swansea and Cardiff, the two main ports, worked to develop those industries above others. Temperance and taxes took their tolls, especially the Excise Tax of 1823 that banned small stills, while the surrounding giants—England, Ireland, and Scotland—were developing their distilling operations to industrial levels.

A slight revival came in 1890, when Frongoch Distillery opened in Bala, a mountainous mining region in the north. It employed 30 workers, who produced 150,000 gallons of whisky in a good year. In 1895, they received a royal warrant from Queen Victoria, making theirs the Royal Welsh Whisky. But by 1910, they pulled up stakes and closed—a shame because an ad for their whisky nicely captures the Welsh attitude toward drinking: "Welsh Whisky is the most wonderful Whisky that ever drove the skeleton from the feast, or painted landscapes in the brain of man. It is the mingled souls of Peat and Barley washed white with the waters of Tryweryn. In it, you will find the sunshine and shadow that chased each other over the billowy fields." It goes on from there, justifying why you always should visit a pub with friends.

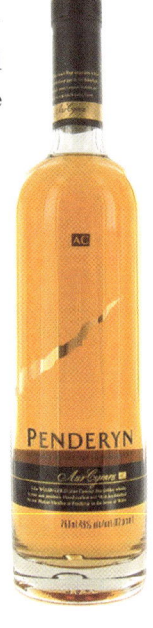

It was in a pub in 1999 that a few friends had the idea of starting the first whisky facility in Wales in nearly a century. In 2004, Penderyn Distillery opened in Brecon Beacons National Park. Started with the great Dr. Jim Swan, Einstein of Whisky, as their master distiller, they installed a unique set of stills by Michael Faraday that creates a highly estery spirit to age in a variety of casks: Madeira, port, bourbon, and sherry. They now boast an all-woman distilling team and have broken open the world whisky category.

Others followed. Dà Mhìle, Aber Falls, the Welsh Wind, and Dyfi have opened, mostly to domestic markets. But in the near future, they all may end up following the lead of countryman Evan Williams by spreading out—except this time, they'll already have a finished bottle of whisky in their hands.

FARM DISTILLERIES RETURN TO SCOTLAND

From earliest days, the crofter, or tenant farmer, has shaped the whisky environment of Scotland. Since the 1700s, the Walker family had owned land near Cupar, between Glenrothes and Dundee, that the Cuthbert family had been working as tenant farmers since the early 1900s. In 1984, Francis Cuthbert and brother Ian bought the family's Lowland farm from the Walker family and grew barley for distilleries, including The Macallan. On the property, the "daft" old water mill hadn't been used for more than one hundred years, and the story goes that, at the start of World War II, locals removed the mill stones to prevent the Nazis from using it in case of invasion. In the early 2000s, Francis got the idea to turn the ancient stone barns of the old mill into Daftmill Distillery.

Like his ancestors, Cuthbert can cycle through the vicissitudes of barley strains and their shifting value to the distiller. As with automobiles, barley varies in terms of fashion and use. An early industry strain developed carcinogenic properties during distillation. The prevalence of beta-glucans in another clogged throughput, adding time to mashing and drainage. Distillers cycled through Golden Promise, Chariot, Optic, Oxbridge, and others before settling into Laurette and Sassy. As researchers develop new strains, they always have the same goal: good yield, meaning how much alcohol a ton of grain can produce, while producing the right flavors and not harming the environment.

The barley for Daftmill comes from the Cuthberts' fields and the water from the well on the property. In 2018, they bottled their first distillation, from 2005, a 12-year-old single malt aged in first-fill, ex-bourbon barrels. On a two-season basis, winter and summer, they continue to bottle vintage and batch releases, working around spring planting and fall harvest. They've created single-cask releases from each year since 2006. As this book is

Digital Age

going to press, they *could* release their first 18-year, "but we don't have plans to do that right now."

Their spent grains, spent lees, and pot ale are used to feed local cattle and nurture their crops, as their forebearers did in harmony with nature. But unlike their ancestors, their whisky, though limited and in demand, can be found everywhere—except that first release, which Francis describes as "rarer than rocking-horse shit."

THE LEGEND OF POPCORN SUTTON

AS A WAY TO MAKE WHISKEY, "MOONSHINE" IS A MISNOMER. Lovingly described as "mountain dew," it went by "poitín" in Ireland and "nip" in Scotland. The tin and copper stills of Scots-Irish and German immigrants traveled with them to North America, where they cooked on moonless nights, all the better for a cloudy sky to obscure the smoke, keeping them safe from thieves and revenue agents. Unaged, untaxed, and unregulated, it formed part of the American experience, from New England, through New Jersey, and into Pennsylvania, since the 1700s. But it came into its own and found its spiritual home in the Appalachian Mountains.

As the craft distilling movement grew in the aughts, moonshine got a second life. Hundreds of new distillers reached back to the romance of rebelliousness and christened their unaged whiskey "moonshine." Odds are that none had heard of Marvin "Popcorn" Sutton then. He grew up in the hollows of the North Carolina mountains, near the border with Tennessee, the beating heart of Appalachia. Legend has it that, sometime in the 1960s, he got drunk in a local tavern and took a pool cue to a malfunctioning popcorn machine. As a result, "Popcorn" became his lifelong moniker.

An authentic, fourth-generation mountain moonshiner, he frequently found himself in trouble with the law in one form or another: assault with a deadly weapon, selling untaxed liquor, possessing unlicensed distilling equipment. Each time, he avoided a lengthy prison sentence, cut a deal on probation, and returned to the hills to resume his trade. But two opposing events cemented the legend of Popcorn Sutton and his "likker."

In 2008, agents from the Bureau of Alcohol, Tobacco, and Firearms uncovered nearly one thousand gallons of his hooch in Tennessee and North Carolina. This transgression set off a new round of indictments, court appearances, a guilty verdict, and a scheduled sentence. At the same time, Jeremy Grosser, a former professional motocross racer and entrepreneur, approached Sutton. His message: Everything that Sutton had been doing

undercover in the hills had become legal, and people were making money from it. Sutton responded, "My likker's always been too good for Mason jars," and signed a deal with Grosser's JM Concepts to distill and market Popcorn Sutton's XXX Tennessee Whiskey. But Sutton had a secret. In addition to battling emphysema, he received a cancer diagnosis. His future didn't look promising.

While Grosser collected investors to bring Sutton's moonshine to the masses, the federal government, the trial judge, and Popcorn's public defender negotiated his sentence from 24 months in federal prison to 18. But Sutton knew that, in his condition, he'd never survive even the shortest time in jail. A mountain man, a proud hillbilly, he had been raised to take control of his own life without help from others. On the night of March 16, 2009, a few days before his scheduled surrender to deputies to begin serving his sentence, Sutton walked into his garage, started up his old Ford Fairmont, and sat in the front seat. Hours later, his wife, Pam, found him slumped over in the front seat, dead.

On the market, Popcorn Sutton's Tennessee White Whiskey was hit and miss. In 2023, Ole Smokey Distillery in Gatlinburg, Tennessee, in conjunction with Sutton's widow, announced that they would create and market two Sutton brands, a bourbon and a white "likker," to honor the legacy of one of America's authentic moonshine heroes. Just leave the Mason jar at home.

Digital Age

THE QUEST OF SHACKLETON'S WHISKY

IN 1908, INTREPID EXPLORER ERNEST SHACKLETON FAILED TO REACH the South Pole, coming within a hundred miles of his goal. The treachery of the polar climate and topography forced him to abandon the expedition, but he succeeded in getting his entire team safely back to Britain, which acclaimed him as a hero. But in one of his base camps, he left behind three crates of Scotch whisky, still in their original paper and straw packaging, which the elements soon covered.

In 2010, conservators of the Antarctic Heritage Trust, based in New Zealand, found the crates as well as two others that held brandy. They carefully extracted one crate from the ice, flying it to a purpose-built environment in New Zealand for careful thawing and to undergo chemical analysis. That was when Indian real estate billionaire Vijay Mallya contacted them.

Shackleton had left behind Mackinlay's Rare Old Highland Malt Whisky, a

family-owned brand established in 1815 that stayed in the family until the 1960s. After several changes in ownership, it found a home with Scottish blending house Whyte and Mackay, makers of The Dalmore, which Mallya owned. Richard Paterson, master blender of Whyte and Mackay and a third-generation "nose," had a brilliant idea: Re-create the whisky that Shackleton left behind and relaunch the once-popular Mackinlay brand.

In 2011, after a series of "delicate conversations" with the trust, they agreed to sample three bottles. The analysis was painstaking: dim lights, white gloves, long needles piercing the corks to extract a specific amount of liquid, a special sealant for the holes. Paterson dis-

covered that the whisky, smoked with peat from the Orkney Islands, had aged in ex-sherry casks of American oak. It took weeks of marrying and blending a range of current single malts to get the replication right, and even in Paterson's masterful hands, the task tested every skill. In the end, he created another masterpiece: Mackinlay's Shackleton Rare Old Malt Whisky, a blended malt containing whiskies from 8 to 30 years, some from the Glen Mhor distillery, the original Mackinlay distillery, which had closed in the 1980s.

From discovery to replication took five years. The original Shackleton release—because two more variations followed—consisted of 50,000 bottles and sold at approximately US $125 each. From each sale, 5 percent went to the Antarctic Heritage Trust. Conservators rewrapped the unearthed bottles, including the samples, in their original packaging and placed them back into their crate. Returned to the icy permafrost of Antarctica, they wait for the next intrepid experiment a hundred years from now.

Digital Age

I WANT MY MGP

THOMAS JEFFERSON NEVER FAVORED THE EXCISE TAX THAT RIVAL Alexander Hamilton convinced Congress to pass in 1791. A laissez-faire capitalist, Jefferson preferred small cottage industries and family farms. Hamilton, an avowed Federalist, believed that a strong, centralized government would protect citizens against the whims of fortune and that taxes should bankroll that protection. As one of his first acts as president, Jefferson rescinded the tax that sparked the Whiskey Rebellion, and distilleries opened throughout the new nation as a result.

In the early 1800s, a few of them opened in Lawrenceburg, on the Indiana side of the Ohio River, across from the new state of Kentucky. George Ross opened one in 1847, and while the quality proved undoubtedly good, the location—on the main passageway to the West and the port of New Orleans—was a stroke of genius. The distillery of Ross and that of his close neighbor, W. P. Squibb, grew into massive alcohol factories that carried them through and beyond the 1800s, until Prohibition shut them down.

At Repeal, Rossville Distillery had its next big upswing. The Seagram company, owned by Canadian Sam Bronfman, eyed it as a central player in its quest to dominate the whiskey category. Bronfman upgraded the equipment to several massive column stills, imposing strict quality control and manufacturing efficiencies. Producing multiple mash bills, the Lawrenceburg plant became the beating heart of his global operation. One of its primary products was an intensely spicy rye whiskey for blending that used only 5 percent barley, just enough to facilitate the necessary sugar conversion.

It went into numerous whiskey products there, including Seagram's 7 Crown, America's favorite then.

In 2000, Seagram imploded, and the distillery went up on the block again. Whiskey was still suffering worldwide, its renaissance not yet begun. French giant Pernod Ricard picked it up, then sold it to CL Financial, owners of Angostura, who renamed it Lawrenceburg Distillers Indiana (LDI), which sold it to Midwest Grain Products (MGP), a Kansas company. During that time, something began to stir. A new generation of distillers and brand owners was rediscovering the joys of rye whiskey. They began sourcing the aged barrels to bottle. The list of whiskeys saying "Distilled in Indiana" on the back label grew long.

Now owned by Luxco and renamed Ross & Squibb, this distillery introduced our palates to the challenge and pleasures of the "Pennsylvania style" 95/5 rye/barley. Intense, spicy, floral, and rich, it landed the perfect punch in the mouth that drinkers were craving after two decades of jet-fuel vodka and Christmas tree gin.

In 2010, Dave Schmier created the Redemption brand to "redeem" the rye of old that fell from favor. He didn't distill but instead sourced, blended, and bottled as he competed with megacompanies in Kentucky and elsewhere. In many ways, he followed the exact playbook that Thomas Jefferson imagined the world should be reading from.

LIQUID GENEALOGY

THE NAMES OF MANY WHISKEY BRANDS LEAD US BACK TO THEIR origins. John Dewar and Jack Daniel; Hiram Walker and John Walker; John Jameson and Jim Beam; all those men existed, plus Wiser, Teacher, and Seagram. Both Overholt and Crow grew old. Trace each one, and you'll find whiskey's commercial beginnings in the 1700s and 1800s. After Prohibition, a slew of new names honored those pulling the industry back together: Albert Blanton, Elmer T. Lee, Jimmy Russell, and Pappy Van Winkle. Henry McKenna,

Evan Williams, and Elijah Craig also emerged, with tenuous relationships to the brands that they represent today. Only recently did we learn about Nathan Green's importance, and William Gooderham resurfaced after a hundred-year slumber.

Savvy marketers know that, for booze, we're hooked on history. The Scots focus on common Gaelic names for ancient places: Balvenie ("village of luck"), Glenmorangie ("vale of the big meadow by the water"), and Balblair ("settlement on the plain"). The Japanese prize the honor in traditional corporate names: Nikka and Suntory. The Irish balance being "new" alongside Jameson and Bushmills. Americans like old men. On a bottle, put the name and bearded face of some guy from history, and you've got a fair shot at success.

In the early days of the whiskey renaissance, consumers had a mild authenticity hangover. With smartphones in hand, they felt compelled to track down the most obscure minutiae, even label glue. ("Is that the *same* glue they used in 1854?") Initially sourced from large, existing distilleries, many of those revival brands made delicious whiskeys, but drinkers almost derailed their enjoyment because they were operating under the false impression that they were smarter than their desires.

But people love their brands, identify with them, glom onto their stories, feel safe and secure with those they know and like—and new ones appear every day, some using personal history, a tried-and-true technique. The Teelings in Ireland and the Nelsons in Tennessee dedicated their futures to reviving their family names and brands, but each had to source whiskey elsewhere before theirs was ready to bottle.

Born in 1772 in County Monaghan, Ireland, Michael Hughes emigrated and eventually settled in Bedford County, Pennsylvania. His son John Joseph enlarged the family farm distillery and purchased a grist mill. Years later, he in turn sold the distilling business to sons Patrick and Francis. There, they produced Belle of Bedford pure rye whiskey until Prohibition spelled the end of the business. Cyrus Kehyari is a great-great grandson of John Joseph Hughes. In 2011, Kehyari picked up the family reins and began his own whiskey quest. His 95/5 rye mash bill for the revived Belle of Bedford Straight Rye brand has been aging in custom casks for 6 and 10 years. The Belle on the label evokes the Victorian age and was family matriarch Cathrine Hughes, but Kehyari's mission represents the most modern of whiskey's endeavors.

ANGEL'S ENVY, A BOURBON EX-PORT

IN THE EARLY DAYS OF THE WATER OF LIFE, WHISKEY WAS ALWAYS flavored. Quickly mashed, it passed once through a crude distillation device, and the result inevitably tasted sulfurous, harsh, and hot. It functioned as a solvent, however, and distillers learned to soak the roots, berries, and herbs of pharmacology in it to extract their essential oils, which made it palatable. Over centuries, that flavoring came from the wooden barrels that carried it, specifically oak, which imparted agreeable flavors and colors.

In the 1800s, wine negotiants trafficked in fortified wines, including sherry and port, which influenced the Scotch and Irish whiskeys that matured in those various barrels. In the 1990s, Balvenie and Glenmorangie became interested in "finishing" their whisky: maturing it in ex-bourbon oak and giving it additional time in a barrel that contained something different. At this time, sherry butts had become more expensive, and bourbon barrels achieved the initial maturation. This new kind of finishing reclaimed some of the "sherry-ness" of old-school Scotch and added market differentiation. Its success spawned imitation.

But American whiskey? "Hell" and "no," came the reply. In the late 1800s and early 1900s, with the Bottled in Bond Act and the Pure Food and Drug Act, the rules for bourbon, rye, and wheat whiskey became more codified and restrictive. The idea of "purity" defined the category. After Repeal and World War II, the Code of Federal Regulations drew a tighter circle around each definition. Bourbon, rye, and wheat were sacrosanct and not to be corrupted. One new, charred barrel, and that was it.

Digital Age

After Lincoln Henderson, master distiller of Brown-Forman, retired, his son Wes Henderson looked for a project that he and his father could work on together. But it had to be something exciting enough to pull his dad from retirement. During his time working on the Jack Daniel's and Woodford Reserve brands, Lincoln had overseen many experiments in maturation. They produced interesting results, but Brown-Forman, a conservative company, had an unofficial motto: "Don't mess with Jack." Many of Lincoln Henderson's experiments never saw the light of day. For him—trained organoleptically as a chemist and influenced by his knowledge of wine and Scotch—taking a standard bourbon profile and tweaking it felt like a natural progression. For Wes, a serial entrepreneur, creating a brand with market differentiation stood foremost in his mind.

In 2011, the debut of Angel's Envy shocked more than just bourbon's old guard. Anyone with less experience and stature than Lincoln Henderson couldn't have pulled it off. Lincoln set the framework for development and threw Wes into the deep end to create the flavor profiles. When asked about using ex-port barrels for finishing them, Wes admits, "We would have liked a story about getting the barrels from monks on a mountaintop, but really, I had a guy in Portugal who was able to get good barrels consistently." Their success has spawned imitation.

A GLASS OF MILK

AN INNOCENT WHISKEY TASTING CAN INSPIRE SANE PEOPLE TO LOSE their senses and open a distillery themselves. In 2000, it happened in Washington, DC, for Rick Wasmund of Copper Fox Distilling, an early pioneer of the American craft movement. Lightning soon struck again at St. Andrews University where, after attending a series of tastings there, Francis Cuthbert decided to open Daftmill in Scotland.

It happened to Gal Kalkshtein in an unlikely place: Tel Aviv, Israel, a country with no whisky tradition. Distilling brandy would have made sense because the country has a robust wine industry; Israelis widely enjoy arak, distilled from grapes and anise seed; and, yes, distillation originated in this area of the world thousands of years ago. But whiskey making, especially single malts, was unheard of. On top of that, Israelis describe themselves as an "impatient" people, and good whiskey needs time to mature. It looked like Kalkshtein's idea was going nowhere fast.

To make matters worse, his friend Tal Chotiner, who was conducting tastings for Diageo, told him not to do it. Barley doesn't grow easily in Israel; the weather isn't suitable for distilling and maturation; and, again, good distilling requires patience. Chotiner pleaded, "It's easier to buy a glass of milk than the whole cow," but his warning fell on deaf ears. Kalkshtein wanted to pioneer whiskey distilling in Israel. Besides, as he says, "If you want an Israeli to do anything, just tell him he can't."

In 2012, Kalkshtein teamed up with Chotiner and distiller Tomer Goren to create Milk & Honey, Israel's first whisky distillery. They then reached out to legendary Dr. Jim Swan, Einstein of Whisky and an international expert in climatic distillation. (Geographically speaking, Israel has five climates, from below sea level to the mountain deserts.) The team decided to use primarily red wine barrels from kosher Israeli wineries. The country never had a whisky distillery, so it also had no regulations. They adopted Scotland's: 100 percent malted barley, a minimum of three years in oak casks, produced in Israel.

The country's lack of distilling heritage also created havoc with the local government and fire department, neither of which had regulations to cover the site—not to mention the rabbis. As Kalkshtein joked, "The Tel Aviv rabbinate isn't kosher enough for Jerusalem or Brooklyn," and as Chotiner's father warned him, "Between two Jews, you have seven opinions." For a sherry-cask finish, they went to Spain and created a kosher sherry using American oak.

In 2023, M&H Elements, their single malt, won the coveted World's Best Single-Malt Whisky Award, and they have won other prestigious industry awards since then. Without a national tradition, they let innovation and experimentation guide them, having learned the virtue of patience.

JAPANESE STRAIGHT FLUSH

IN SOPHIA COPPOLA'S 2003 MOVIE, *LOST IN TRANSLATION*, BILL MURRAY as Bob Harris utters the famous line, "Make it Suntory time." A decade later, when Yamazaki won a prestigious international whisky award, few people made the connection. But the news broke into the wider world, which the newswires picked up, spawning a thousand magazine, newspaper, and blog articles. After 90 years, Japanese whisky was having its close-up moment.

In 2012, after years of delays, Nikka, Japan's second-largest whisky maker, received final approval to enter the American market. In the whisky community, Suntory and Nikka brands were flying off shelves and over bars. Whisky enthusiasts were discovering smaller Japanese companies, as well. One of those was operated by Ichiro Akuto and his distillery at Chichibu Distillery. But Akuto's story tells the account of this discovery in an unlikely form.

Like many whisky stories in Japan, it begins with family, in this case one who ran a sake-brewing business started in 1625. In the mid-1940s, Isoji Akuto, Ichiro's grandfather, started distilling whisky in pot stills and a continuous still purchased from Scotland. The postwar influx of American soldiers triggered a whiskey boom, and distilleries strived to make "local" whisky, meaning an inexpensive mix of grain spirits and imported whisky, to satisfy the demand. In 1983, Suntory reportedly sold 12 million cases of whisky, most of it destined for the mizuwari, a highball drink. That year, Isoji Akuto replaced his stills with Japanese pot stills and switched to making all-malt whiskies. At his Hanyu Distillery, he blended "high-character" malt whisky and imported Scotch whisky under the Golden Horse brand.

The 1980s and '90s were unkind to whiskey production all over the world, however, including Japan, and Hanyu ceased production in 2000, selling to new owners who didn't want to continue making whisky. Assets included four hundred hogsheads and puncheons of malt whisky that Ichiro eventually had to buy back from the new owner. In doing so,

he launched a line of whiskies that had collectors whispering in awe: the vaunted Card Series.

In 2004, Akuto founded Chichibu Distillery, the first new Japanese distillery in more than 30 years, and the next year began releasing the Card Series. Initially blended from only four barrels, each bottling took the name of a suit in a deck of cards: diamonds, clubs, spades, and hearts. Demand quickly increased. Over a period of nine years, Akuto carefully blended and finished the barrels of malt whisky into 54 different variations, each illustrated with the face from a standard deck of playing cards, plus two jokers. Collectors acquired the bottles, traded them, blogged about them, and stampeded them into unicorn status.

That stampede launched Akuto and Chichibu into the next realm of Japanese whisky makers, from a small craft startup to a larger facility that opened in 2019. Over his shoulder, his late grandfather guides his hand and heart as Chichibu innovates the future.

AMPHORAE OF ATHYR

AROUND THE WORLD, MAKERS OF MALT WHISKEY FACE THE CONUN-
drum of copying their Scottish muses or tweaking the process to highlight what makes their products unique. Many times, the result tastes almost indistinguishable. But in Lebanon, a choice forced on a maker resulted in a stunningly unique variation that called into service an artifact of antiquity that once measured civilization's progress: the clay amphora.

Dating to 1839, Roy Riachi's family winery and distillery sits in the Khenchara highlands overlooking Beirut. Riachi had his grandfather's old Armagnac alembic and distilling equipment and saw an opportunity to add a new product to the product line, a Lebanese single-malt whisky, Athyr, meaning "otherworldly." He sourced barley from the Bekaa Valley, and then malting on the winery roof, in the intense Mediterranean sun, which gave it a sense of place. But maturing the whisky in barrels of local oak ran into an unusual problem. Lebanon prohibits cutting down any live forest tree that doesn't bear fruit.

To circumvent this challenge, Riachi reached into history, before the ancient Celts fashioned watertight wooden casks, to clay amphorae. Made from local terracotta clay, the amphorae he uses are fired in a kiln in a nearby village. "The terracotta is porous and breathable, much like concrete," says Riachi, which allows for some interaction between the liquid and the environment. But a clever reading of the logging ban gives the whisky access to maturation with wood, a global standard for flavor. Lebanon forbids cutting down the oak tree—but not pruning it. Riachi debarks limbs and cures them in the sun for nearly three years to leech

the tightly bound tannins that would cause bitterness. In kilns, they toast to specific degrees before going into amphorae ranging from 80 to 180 liters. Slow maturation, between 6 and 10 years in cool cellars dug into hillsides, allows uniquely earthy, rich flavors to develop. Cedarwood, one of Athyr's releases goes a step further. Riachi dumps the clay pots and oak and reintroduces the whisky with small staves of toasted cedar for about a year, highlighting the unique spice and oakiness that lives up to its otherworldliness. "In Lebanon, cedar isn't even allowed to be pruned, so we have to forage for broken pieces," Riachi admits, giving his labor an added dimension of rigor and patience. First distilled in 2013, with no coloring and no chill filtering, bottled in 2019 at amphora strength (between 54 and 57% ABV), and available in limited batches, Athyr harnesses ancient culture to demonstrate what the future of whisky can achieve.

ACKNOWLEDGMENTS

Henry Preiss
Ewan Gunn
Maria Coelho
Dianne Greene
Claire Henderson
Christine J. McCafferty
Alia Campbell
Cory McCauley
Matt Higgins
Nick Laracuente
Sam Komlenic
Aaron Hollis
Patrick Bochy
Pam Curtain
Jonathan Goldstein
Simon Brooking
Mark Reynier
Jonathan Driver
Andrew McKenzie Smith
Cutter Davis
Dave Mitton
Tim Master
Francis Cuthbert
Mike Harrison
Sophie Cawthorne
Jean Harrison
Amir Peay
Drew Kulsveen
Patrick Barry
Robert Athol
Caitlin Bartlemay
Jana Meyer
Michelle Flores
Joe Whittaker
Charles Nelson
Bill Lark
David Vitale
Andy Fairgrieve
Dave Mulligan
William Keeler
F. Paul Pacult
Dave Singh

Charlie Rodman
Todd Leopold
Charles Merinoff
Jeremy Shephard
Tish Harcus
Steve Beam
Steve Bashore
Laura Fields
Richard Paterson
Gregg Glass
Yumi Yoshikawa
Ichiro Acuto
Brian Kinsman
Gregory Fitch
Liz Brusca
Kelley Spillane
Donna Hibbert
Mark Edwin Andrews III
Timothy Holtz
Steve Jones
Bill Lumsden
Steve Henderson
Jena Ellenwood
Larry Kass
Lauren Newcomb
Jeff Crowe
Tal Chotiner
Gal Kalkshtein
Tomer Goren
Raj Sabharwal
Ashok Chokalingam
J. Rosser Lomax
Tim Knittel
Shirley Harmon
Stephen Lyman
Christopher Pellegrini
Stephen Duffy
Jen Marshall
Nicole Austin
Eryn Reece
David Stirk
Roy Riachi

Jessica Davis
Malcolm Waring
Jota Tanaka
Angela D'Orazio
Wes Henderson
Chris Corbin
Philip Duff
Ferdinand Meyer
Don Livermore
Michael Martello
Zach Sinclair
Kelly Kenneally
Rob Sherman
Susannah Jaggers
Ray Lafferty
The Islay Museum
Joe Magliocco
Lillie Pierson
Alisa Stratton
Manuela Savonna
Eleanor Judge
Sophia Weldon
Phoebe Carr
Margaret Wilson
Paul McLaughlin
Britney Hupp
Christine Cooney
Carol Quinn
Aoife Geraghty
Jenna McIntosh
Michelle Glancy
Zev Glesta
Michael Veach
Patrick Moniz
Jack Sullivan
Fionnán O'Connor
Alan Goldstein
Dave Burkhart
Hishiroku Koji Maker
Gary Spedding
Toshio Ueno
Lasse Vesterby

Acknowledgments

BIBLIOGRAPHY

BOOKS

Ambrose, William M. *Bluegrass Prohibition: Prohibition in Lexington, Fayette County, Kentucky 1920–1934*. Lexington, KY: William M. Ambrose, 2010.

Arthur, Helen. *A Teacher's Tale*. Bristol, UK: Allied Domecq Spirits and Wines (UK) Limited, 2005.

Barnard, Alfred. *The Whisky Distilleries of the United Kingdom. Harper's Weekly Gazette*, 1887. Edinburgh: Reprinted by Berlinn Publishing, 1969.

Boles Elison, Betty. *Illegal Odyssey: 200 Years of Kentucky Moonshine*. Bloomington, IL: 1st Book Library (Author House), 2003.

Brousseau, Chris. Story of The Glenlivet. Internal essay from the Chivas Bros. Ltd. 2023.

Brown, Jim; Reps, Louis. *The Rise and Fall of Pattisons Whisky of Leith*. Skövd, Sweden: REPSpect AB, 2020.

Buhner, Stephen Harrod. *Sacred and Herbal Healing Beers*. Boulder, CO: Siris Books, Brewer's Association, 1998.

Clagett, Marshall. *Ancient Egyptian Science: A Source Book*. Philadelphia: American Philosophical Society, 1989.

Cowdery, Charles K. *Bourbon, Straight: The Uncut and Unfiltered Story of American Whiskey*. Chicago: Made and Bottled in Kentucky, 2004.

Cowdery, Charles K. *The Best Bourbon You'll Never Taste*. Chicago: Made and Bottled in Kentucky, 2012.

Daiches, David. *Scotch Whisky: Its Past and Present*. Edinburgh: Berlinn Limited, 1995

de Kergommeaux, Davin. Canadian Whisky, Updated and Expanded: The Essential Portable Expert (Third Ed.). New York: Appetite–Penguin Random House Canada, 2024.

Downard, William L. *Dictionary of the History of the American Brewing and Distilling Industries*. Westport, CT: Greenwood Press, 1980.

FitzGerald, Augustine. *The Letters of Synesius of Cyrene*. Translated into English with Introduction and Notes. London: Oxford University Press: Humphrey Milford, 1926.

Fleischman, Joseph. *The Art of Blending and Compounding Liquors and Wines*. New York: Dick & Fitzgerald, 1886. Reprint by Kessinger Publishing. Whitefish, MT: 2010.

Forbes, R. J. *Short History of the Art of Distillation: From the Beginnings to the Death of Cellier Blumenthal*. Leiden, NL: E. J. Brill, 1948.

Galiano, Martine; Boyer, Phillip. *Chartreuse the Liqueur*. Voiron, FR: Publication Chartreuse, 2019.

Garnham, Amanda; Bradfer, Alain. Armagnac Academies: Armagnac Spirit. Bureau National Interprofessionel de l'Armagnac (BNIA) Condom, FR: Suds-Concepts Presse & Edition, 2012.

Gately, Iain. *Drink: A Cultural History of Alcohol*. New Hyde Park, NY: Avery Publishing, 2009.

Haara, Brian F. *Bourbon Justice: How Whiskey Law Shaped America*. Lincoln: University of Nebraska Press, 2018.

Heimann, Jim; Heller, Steven. *Alcohol and Tobacco: 100 Years of Stimulating Ads*. Cologne, DE: Taschen GmbH, 2022.

Heron, Craig. *Booze*. Roseville, MN: Between the Lines Publishing, 2003.

Hill, Rev. George. *An Historical Account of the Plantation in Ulster at the Commencement of the Seventeenth Century, 1608–1620*. Belfast: M'Caw, Stevenson & Orr, 1877.

History of Tennessee. Nashville: Goodspeed Publishing Co., 1886.

Isenberg, Nancy. *White Trash: The 400-Year Untold History of Class in America*. New York: Viking Press, 2016.

Jackson, Michael. *The Whiskies of Scotland: Encounters of a Connoisseur*. London: Watkins Publishing, 1999.

Jackson, Michael. *Whiskey: The Definitive World Guide*. New York: DK Publishing, 2005.

Jameson, John and Son. *Truths About Whisky*. London: Sutton Sharpe and Co., 1879.

Klein, Arthur. "The Whiskey Ring." Masters Essay, Columbia University, 1909.

Lebel, Frederic. The Quintessence of Armagnac. Translated from French by Amanda Garnham. Paris: cherche medi, 2011

Leyburn, James G. *The Scotch Irish*. Chapel Hill: University of North Carolina Press, 1989.

Livermore, Don. *The Keeper of History*. Windsor: Walkerville Publishing, Inc., 2022

Lucas, A.; Harris, J. *Ancient Egyptian Materials and Industries*. Mineola, NY: Dover Publications, 2012.

MacLean, Charles, ed. *Know-It-All Whiskey*. New York: Quarto Group, an imprint of Wellfleet Press, 2017.

Martin, Angus. *Campbeltown Whisky: An Encyclopedia*. Edinburgh, Scotland: The Grimsay Press, 2020.

McDonald, Gen. John. *Secrets of the Great Whiskey Ring: Containing a Complete Exposure of the Illicit Whiskey Frauds Culminating in 1875, and the Connections of Grant, Babcock, Douglass, Chester H. Krum, and Other Administration Officials, Established by Positive and Unequivocal Documentary Proofs*. Chicago: Belford, Clarke & Co., 1880. Creative Media Partners, LLC. 2023.

McDonnell, Duggan. *Drinking the Devil's Acre*. San Francisco: Chronicle Books, 2017.

McGuire, E. B. Irish Whiskey: A History of Distilling, the Spirit Trade and Excise Controls in Ireland. Dublin: Gill & Macmillan, 1973.

McNicoll, David. *The Language of Whisky*. Brooklyn: Wheatfield Press, 2020.

Minnick, Fred. *Bourbon: The Rise, Fall, and Rebirth of an American Whiskey*. Dover, MN: Voyageur Press, 2016

Mitenbuler, Reid. *Bourbon Empire*. New York: Penguin Books, 2016.

Moss, Michael S.; Hume, John R. *The Making of Scotch Whisky: A History of* the Scotch Whisky Distilling Industry. Edinburgh: James & James; New York: Crane, Russak & Co., 1981.

O'Connor, Fionnán. *A Glass Apart: Irish Single Pot Still Whiskey*. Chadstone, AU: The Images Publishing Group Pty, Ltd. 2017.

Okrent, Daniel. *Last Call: The Rise and Fall of Prohibition*. New York: Simon and Schuster, Scribner, 2010.

Rennick, Robert M. *Kentucky Place Names*. Lexington: The University Press of Kentucky, 1984.

Rives, F. & J.; Bailey, George A. *The Congressional Globe: Third Session, Fortieth Congress*. Washington, DC, 1869.

Ronnberg, Ami, ed. *The Book of Symbols*. Cologne, DE: Taschen GmbH, 2010.

Roob, Alexander. *Alchemy and Mysticism*. Cologne, DE: Taschen Bibliotheca Universalis, 1997.

Sismondo, Christine. *America Walks into a Bar: A Spirited History of Taverns and Saloons, Speakeasies and Grogshops*. London: Oxford University Press, 2011.

Standage, Tom. *A History of the World in 6 Glasses*. New York: Walker Publishing Company, 2006.

Taketsuru, Masataka. *On the Production Methods of Pot Still Whisky, May 1920*. Translated from the Japanese by Ruth Anne Herd. Edinburgh: humming earth, an imprint of Zeticula Ltd, 2021.

The Repertory of Patent Inventions and Other Discoveries and Improvements in Arts, Manufactures and Agriculture, vol. 8. London: T. and C. Underwood, 1830.

Webb, James. *Born Fighting: How the Scots-Irish Shaped America*. New York: Crown Publishing, 2005.

Weisfeld, Jerrod. "The Whiskey Ring and the Men Behind It." Masters essay, Columbia University, 1937.

Winkler, Allan M. "Whiskey West of the Appalachians: Drinking on the American Frontier." Masters Essay, Columbia University, 1967.

Young, Al. *Four Roses: The Return of a Whiskey Legend*. Louisville, KY: Butler Books, 2010.

Zoeller, Chet. *Bourbon In Kentucky*. Louisville: Butler Books, 2009.

Zoeller, Chet. *Kentucky Whiskey Barons*. Louisville: Butler Books, 2014.

PLACES

- Oscar Getz Museum, Bardstown, KY
- Pernod Ricard/Hiram Walker distillery private archives, Windsor, Canada
- Rochester Historical Society, Library, Rochester, NY
- Filson Historical Society, Louisville, KY
- Buffalo Trace Distillery, Frankfort, KY
- Frazier History Museum, Louisville, KY
- Evan Williams Bourbon Experience, Louisville, KY
- James B. Beam Distilling Co., Clermont, KY
- Johnnie Walker Scotch Whiskey Experience, Edinburgh, Scotland

- Jameson Bow Street Distillery, Dublin, Ireland
- National Museum of Scotland, Edinburgh, Scotland
- Metropolitan Museum of Art, New York, NY
- Surgeon's Hall Museum, Edinburgh, Scotland

ONLINE AND OTHER MEDIA

McKinnon, Tanya Lynn. "The Historical Geography of the Distilling Industry in Ontario: 1850–1900." Wilfrid Laurier University, 2000.

"The Seagram Company, Ltd." International Directory of Company Histories. Encyclopedia.com.

Rich, H. S. & Company. "The Western Brewer: And Journal of the Barley, Malt and Hop Trades. Rich, H. S. & Company, January 1912.

Morry, Emily. "For the Cure: The Story of Duffy's Pure Malt Whiskey, Pt. 2." Rochester Public Library Rochester Historical Society.

Sanneh, Kelefa. "Reinventing Scotch Whisky: Letter from Islay." *The New Yorker*, February 3, 2013.

"The Stein Family." The Kennetpans Trust. September 5, 2019.

"The Haig Family Story." The Kennetpans Trust. December 30, 2010.

"The Jameson Family Story." The Kennetpans Trust. December 30, 2010.

Platt, Richard. "Buying the Contraband." Smugglers' Britain, 2006.

Andrew Thomson, "Seagram, Joseph Emm." Dictionary of Canadian Biography, vol. 14. University of Toronto/Université Laval, 2003.

Fortune Editors. "Who Is Publicker?" *Fortune*, November 1933.

Guido, George. "Remember When: Schenley Distilling Company Ruled the Roost for Many Years in Gilpin." Valley News Dispatch, Trib Live, November 27, 2022.

Coleman, Kenny, Ryan Cecil, and Fred Minnick, hosts. Bourbon Pursuit (podcast). "E. H. Taylor Despised Stagg and More Bourbon Law with Brian Haara." May 2020, aired April 8, 2022.

DISCUS 2007, Distilled Spirits Council of the United States.

"Bourbon Whiskey/Jacob Spears." Hopewell Museum Bourbon County Historical Markers.

www.Haigwhisky.com.

https://www.referenceforbusiness.com/industries/Food-Kindred-Products/Distilled-Blended-Liquors.html.

Hopewell Museum. https://www.hopewellmuseum.org/learn/historic-preservation/bourbon-county-historical-markers/bourbon-whiskey-jacob-spears.

Sanborn Fire Maps 1895, https://www.loc.gov/item/sanborn09789_001/

www.HistoryNet.com.

www.Beamcompany-histories.com.

www.whiskeyuniv.com

F. R. Allchin. *India: The Ancient Home of Distillation?* University of Cambridge. https://www.jstor.org/stable/2801640.

clan.com, https://clan.com/blog/tradition-of-the-quaich.

Cadenhead's, www.cadenheads.com.

Irish Whiskey, A Story of Irish Whiskey, Audioboom Podcasts

Merchant Bottlers, Company websites

Weir, R. B. "In and Out of Ireland: The Distillers Company Ltd. and the Irish Whiskey Trade 1900–39. Jstor.org, 1980.

http://www.smuggling.co.uk/history_buying.html.

CWRT Congress YouTube, https://youtu.be/x2OGRBdb-cQ.

www.dramdevotees.com.

www.whiskipedia.com.

www.bourbonveach.com.

Carl, Matthew. "Looking Back: Duffy's Pure Malt Whiskey." Looking Back by Matthew Carl. https://leroyheritage.org/looking-back/f/looking-back-duffys-pure-malt-whiskey.

Royal Commission on Whisky and Other Potable Spirits, British Medical Journal 1909.

WhiskeyID, https://whiskeyid.com/stitzel-weller-timeline/.

Enclyclopedia.com, https://www.encyclopedia.com/books/politics-and-business-magazines/seagram-company-ltd.

Japan Inc, https://www.japaninc.com/article.php?articleID=1472.

https://whiskyadvocate.com/what-we-lost-in-the-whisky-loch/.

https://www.etymonline.com/word/booze.

https://www.ohsu.edu/historical-collections-archives/theres-cure-historic-medicines-and-cure-alls-america.

Whiskyscience.blogspot.com.

"S. Bernard and His Foundation," in *The Benedictines of Caldey Island*. The Abbey, Isle of Caldey, 1912, 122. Owner and Tironensian Order: https://archive.org/details/benedictinesofca00isle/page/120/mode/2up?view=theater.

YouTube: The Story of Leopold Bros. Three Chamber Still, YouTube/Todd Leopold. https://www.youtube.com/watch?v=0NL2vimfbog&t=671s.

Straight Up: Kentucky Bourbon, YouTube. https://www.youtube.com/watch?v=i7wXeL5SgTw.

Reps, Louis. *The History of Spirit Safes*. www.glenlochy.com, https://youtu.be/34nT8yv4LcE.

CWRT Congress. *The Whiskey Ring Scandal*. YouTube. https://youtu.be/x2OGRBdb-cQ.

"A Story of Irish Whiskey." Audioboom Podcasts. https://audioboom.com/posts/7268064-revolution-war?playlist_direction=forward.

"Old Overholt: The History of a Whiskey, Part III." Edited and expanded by K. R. Overholt Chritchfield. KarensBranches.com, 1999.

"Annual Report of the Commissioner of Internal Revenue." Fiscal Year Ended June 30, 1887. Washington: Government Printing Office, 1887.

UKV International, Whisky Investment. "A History of Welsh Single Malt Whisky and Welsh Whisky Brands." WhiskyInvestments.com.

Risen, Clay. "Jack Daniel's Embraces a Hidden Ingredient: Help From a Slave." *The New York Times,* 2016.

TheBourbonCulture. "MGP Indiana: Past, Present and Future." BourbonCulture.com.

Cohen, Jason. "The Biggest Distillery You've Never Heard of is in

Lawrenceburg, Indiana." *Cincinnati Magazine,* 2016.

Drake, Bernie. "When Peoria Tried to Monopolize Whiskey." *Peoria Magazine,* nd.

Woolever, Linda. "Living Proof: America's First Whiskey Was Born in Maryland." *Baltimore Magazine,* 2023.

Boyle, Judith. "A Short History of Irish Poitín." RTE Brainstorm, 2023.

CREDITS

Images taken by author unless otherwise specified below.

Amrut Distilleries: 154 (both)
Andrew Kung Photography: xi, 7, 72
Bar 1661: 38
Berry Brothers & Rudd: 199
Brown-Forman Distillery: 118 (both)
Bruichladdich Distillery: 193 (right)
Cadenhead's: 86
Castle Brands: 158, 159 (both)
Chatham Imports: 45 (both)
Compass Box Whisky Company: 185
Courtesy of David Burkhart: 135 (top left and right)
Diageo Group: 62, 68, 69, 70, 79
Disruptive Craft Spirits: 19
Heaven Hill Brands: 56
Heavenly Spirits: 21 (bottom)
Heavenly Spirits Imports: 178
Hishiroku Koji Master: 127 (both)
Honkaku Spirits: 126 (bottom)
Hood River Distillers: 184 (top)
Hotaling & Co.: 182
Hughes Bros. Distillers: 206
International Beverage: 139
Irish Distillers Pernod Ricard: 169 (top), 123, 167 (bottom)
iStock/Amy Sparwasser: 187 (left)
iStock/BalkansCat: 109
iStock/Bitter: viii (bottom)
iStock/Bob Hilscher: 33 (top)
iStock/Daneel85: 165
iStock/Dietmar Rauscher: 73
iStock/Halamka: 40
iStock/JJFarquitectos: 175
iStock/joymsk: 2
iStock/karenfoleyphotography: 195
iStock/Mathilde Audibert: 21 (top)
iStock/memoriesarecaptured: 80
iStock/spaxiax: vi–ix
iStock/whitemay: 31
J.J. Corry: 124
Joshua Feldman, the Coopered Tot: 30, 33 (bottom), 60, 66, 75, 78, 91 (both), 94, 99 (all), 100, 103, 104, 112, 114 (bottom left and right), 133 (both), 140, 141, 149, 151, 153, 161, 162 (all), 163 (all), 166, 168, 169 (bottom), 176, 187 (right), 194, 198, 201, 204, 207
King Car Group: 196
Kirin Brewery Co.: 174
Leopold Bros. Distillery: 188
Lindores Abbey Distillery: 25, 26
M&H Distillery: 209
Mark A. Meggs, volunteer, Falls of the Ohio State Park: 57
Ministry of Rum: 42
Mount Vernon Ladies' Association: 58
Museum of Islay Life: 49
National Museums Scotland: 15, 35
Nelson's Green Brier Distillery: 88, 89
Nikka Whisky Distilling Co.: 76, 77, 146 (right)
Oxmoor Bourbon Company: 129 (both)
Palm Bay International: 173
public domain by Amélie Munier-Romilly: 82
public domain by George Caleb Bingham: 51

public domain by Gilbert Stuart: 59
public domain by Pieter Bruegel the Elder: 18
public domain by Robert Pool and John Cash: 70
public domain by Tommaso da Modena: 10
public domain courtesy of David Burkhart: 134
public domain from Courby Spirits: 142
public domain from James E. Pepper Distilling Co.: 102
public domain from the US Patent and Trademark Office: 117
public domain: 11 (top left, bottom left), 13, 20, 24, 84, 90, 96, 98 (both), 114 (top), 119, 126 (top), 132, 146 (left), 150, 152, 202

Riachi Winery & Distillery: 212, 213
Sagamore Spirit: 136
Sazerac Company: 107, 171
Shutterstock/Sergj: iii
Sotheby's: 143
Starward Distillery: 83
Stauning Whisky: 116 (both), 184 (bottom), 224
Suntory Global Spirits: 145, 148
Venture Whisky: 210, 211
Whyte and Mackay: 203 (bottom left and right)
William Grant and Sons: 164
Winnipeg Tribune Photograph Collection University of Manitoba Archives & Special Collections: 149
Zachary Sinclair via Grizzly Media: 103

INDEX

Aber Falls, 198
Act of Union (1707), 70
An Act to Allow the Bottling of Distilled Spirits in Bond (1897), 128
An Act to Grant Certain Duties of Excise upon Spirits Distilled from Corn or Grain in Scotland and Ireland (1823), 41
Adam, Edouard, 76
Akuto, Ichiro, 210, 211
Akuto, Isoji, 210, 211
Alcohol
  curative powers of hard, xii
  federal administration of, 41
  by volume, 14
Alembic, 10–11
Alexander, John, 119
Alexander, Thomas John, 119
Allen, William, xv, 92
American Brands, 67
American Medicinal Spirits, 103
Amorik, single malt fever and, 184
Amrut, 154, 155, 196
Anabaptism, 44
Anchor Distilling, 182–183
Anderson, James, 58
Andrews, Lavonne, 158
Andrews, Mark Edwin, 158–159
Andrews, Mark III, 160
Angel's Envy, 208
Anglo-Irish Trade War (1930s), 167
Angostura, 205
Anti-temperance efforts, 99
Antrim, 159
Aqua vitae, 44
Archimedes of Syracuse, 14
Armagnac, 10, 21
Ashbury, Herbert, 6

Ashley, H. M., xiii.
  Johnny Bull Machine of, 117–118, 143, 162
Athyr, 212, 213
Austin, Nichole, 12
Australia, prohibition and, 82

Babcock, Orville, 99
Baby Power, 123
Bacon, Francis, 14
Ballantine's, 141
Ballblair, 139
Balmenach, 139
Balvenie, 116, 207
Bán 1661 (poitín), 39
Barnard, Alfred, 55
Barrels
  determining size of, 6–7
  regular, 29
  smuggler's, 29
  swishing, 137
  wooden, 6–7, 7
Barrie, Rachel, 12
Bartles & Jaymes, 152
Bashore, Steve, 59
Bastille 1789, 179
Beam, David, 66, 67
Beam, Jack, 66
Beam, Jacob, family of, 66
Beam, James Beauregard, 67
Beam, Jeremiah, 67
Beam, Jim, xii, 60, 194, 205
  brand of, 67
  decanters of, 163
  inclusion of sour mash in label of, 74–75
Beam family, 60, 66
  distilling dynasty under, xii
Beer, 79
Bell, Arthur, & Sons, 108
Belle Meade, launch of, 89
Belle of Bedford Straight Rye, 206

Ben Nevis Distillery, 177
Berard, Isaac, 76
Bergius, Agnes Teacher, 140–141
Bergius, Walter, 140
Bergius, William, xv, 15
Bernheim, Bernard, 106
Bernheim, Cabin Still, 107
Bernheim, Isaac, 106
Bernheim Distillery, 107, 170
Berry Brothers, 124, 162
Berry Brothers & Rudd, 87, 88. *See also* Cutty Sark
Beveridge, Jim, 185
Bimi, 148
Black Death, 6
Black & White, as brand, 172, 174, 185
Blanton, Albert, 104–105, 205
Blumenthal, Jean Baptiste Cellier, xv, 37, 76
Boehms, 66
Bombergers, 44, 66
Bo'ness, 146
Boone, Daniel, 50–51
Boone, Wattie, 50–51
Booz, E. G., Distillery Company, 85
Booz, Edmund G., 84–85
Bottled in Bond Act (1897), xiii, 41, 102, 122, 128, 188, 207
Bourbon, 128–129
  flat lining of industry, xiii–xix
Bourbon, Evan Williams, 57
Bourbon Pompeii, 105
Bourbon tourism, 105
Bow Street Distillery, 36, 52–54, 54–55, 167
Boyle, Robert, 14
Brandy, 178
Bristow, Benjamin, 99
Bronfman, Charles, 174
Bronfman, Edgar Sr., 174

Bronfman, Samuel, xiii, xiv, 101, 113, 149, 151, 174, 194, 196, 204
Brown, George, 102, 118, 128, 162, 167, 196
Browne, Tom, 62
Brown-Forman, 103
   acquisition of Jack Daniels, 73, 207
Bruegel, Pieter, the Elder, 19
Bruichladdich Distillery, 192–193
Bruno de Cologne, 30
Buchanan's, 164, 183, 185
Budoshu, Daikoku, 160
Buffalo Trace Distillery, 105, 122, 170–171, 194
Bulleit Bourbon, 149
Bulleit Experiences, 107
Bullitt, Alexander Scott, 128–129
Bullitt, Thomas Walker, 128
Bullitt, William Marshall, 129
Burns, Robert, 28
Bushmills, xiv, 33, 159, 167, 206
Butler, Victoria Eady, 91
Byass, Antonio Flores y Silvia, 95
Byass, Gonzalez, 95

Cadenhead, William, independent bottling of, 86–87, 88
Caledonian, 186
Calvert, decanters of, 163
Cambus, 185, 186
Cameronbridge Distillery, 37, 69–70, 78
Cameron Brig, 37
Canadian Club, xiii, 97, 115, 141, 172
Canadian whiskey, xv
Cardhu, 63, 68
Carsebridge, 186, 192
Carthusian Order, 30
Cascade Hollow, 12–13, 73
Castle & Key, 122
Cedarwood, 213
Charcoal filtration, 72–73
Charente, 178
Charles II, King of France, xii, 21, 38

Charlot, 199
Charter Oak, 139
Chateau Montelena, 182
Chemistry, Bureau of, 102
Chichibu Distillery, 210, 211
Chivas Brothers, 88, 149, 183
Chotiner, Tal, 209
Cincinnati Distributing Corporation, 101
Clark Distillers, 159
Classic Malts, 108
Clear Creek Distillers, 184
CL Financial, 205
Clynelish, 63
Coffey, Aeneas, xiii., xv, 28, 37, 62, 64, 77
Coffey Grain Whisky, 77
Coffey stills, 37, 69, 76–77, 78, 92, 147, 176
Cognac, 178
Coleraine, charter of, 32–33
Collier's The National Weekly (magazine), 132
Company store model, 52–53
Compass Box Whiskey, 186
Concentration Act (1922), 103
Connemara (peated Irish whiskey), 177
Continental Distilling, 139
Cooley Distillery, xiv, 160, 176–177, 184
Copper Fox Distilling, 208
Copper Fox Laphroaig, 116
Cor, John, 24, 26
Corby, Henry, 88, 141–142
Corby Wines and Spirits, 141–142
Cork, distillation of, xiv, 159, 176
Correy, J. J., Irish Whiskey of, 124–125
Cowan, Jessie "Rita," 146–147
Cradle Mountain Distillery, 83
Craft whiskey movement, 12–13
Craig, Elijah, 66, 206
Crampton, C. A., 188
Cream of Kentucky, 101
Crow, James, xiii, 74–75, 205
Crown Royal, 113, 149, 151
Cumberland Gap, 50–51

Cumming, Helen, 67–68
Curcurbit, 2
Cuthbert, Francis, 199–200, 208
Cuthbert, Ian, 199
Cutty Sark, 164, 183, 185. *See also* Barry Brothers & Rudd

Daft Distillery, 199
Daftmill Distillery, 199, 208
Dallas Dhu, 192
Dalmore Distillery, 94–95, 202
Daly, B., 159
Da Mhile, 198
Dancourt, Edouard, 179
Daniel, Jack, 74, 89–90, 163, 196, 205, 207
   Brown-Forman acquisition of, 73
   distillery of, 91
   "sour mash" and, 74
D'Armorique elixir, 178
Dartigolongue, 21
Davis, Mortimer, 141–142
d'Estrées, Francois-Hannibal, 30
Devil's Acre, 134
Dewar, John, 205
Dewar, John, & Son, 88, 141
Dewar, John Alexander, 119
Dewar, Thomas John, 119
Dewar, Tommy, xiv, 79, 118, 119–120, 123, 162, 164
"Dewarisms," 120
Dewar scotch, 160, 162, 174, 183, 185
Diageo, xiv, 33, 68, 69, 79, 107, 109, 125, 151, 155, 209
Dickel, George, 73
Dillon, Marshall, 152
Displacement, 14
Distillation, 10, 20, 28, 38, 44, 48, 72–73
Distillation Prohibition Act (1839), 82
Distillers Company Ltd. (DCL), 63, 69, 78–79, 101, 107, 108, 164
Double boiler, 12
Dublin Liberties, 54

Duff, Philip, 19
Duffy, Walter, 104, 122, 132–133
   pure malt whiskey and, 132–133
Dupie, Christophe, 179
Duties on Spirits (Scotland) Act (1814), 71

Early Times brand, 66
Elizabeth II, Queen of England, xiii, 151
Embassy Club, 139
Excise Act (1823), 66, 67, 71
The Excise Officer's Manual (book), 65

Falls of Ohio, 56
Faraday, Michael, 198
Farnsley, Alex, 106, 139, 170
Farnsley, Charlie, 107
Field, Charles Kellogg, 135
Finch, Joseph, distillery of, 60, 100, 101
Forman, Brown, 118
Fornier, J. B., 76
Fortune Brands, 67
Four Roses, 107, 149, 172, 174, 175, 194–195
Fox, James, xv, 64
Frankfort Distillery, 103, 107, 194
Franklin, Lady Jane, 82
Frongoch Distillery, 198
Fuji-Gotemba Distillery, 174
Fuji Single Grain Japanese Whiskey, 175

Gaines, W. A., and Co., 75
Gangs of New York (movie), 6
Gate, St. James, 54
George IV (United Kingdom), 71
George VI (United Kingdom), 151
Giant's Causeway, 33
Gilbey, W. & A., 124, 167
Gilbey's, 108
Gilpin, George, 59
Glaser, John, 185–186
Glass Bottle Trade, 117
Glencoe, 106
Glenfiddich Straight Malt Whisky, xiv, 164–165, 183

Glenkinchie Distillery, 70
Glenlivet, 70–71, 78, 183
Glen Mhor Distillery, 203
Glenmorangle, 59, 207
Glenmore Distillery, 103
Glenora Distillery, 184
Golden Promise, 199
Golden Triangle, 54–55
Golden Wedding Rye, xiv, 100, 101
Gooderham, William, xv, 92, 206
Gooderham & Worts, 80, 92, 93, 141, 142, 149
Gordon, Alexander, 71
Gordon, Charles, 164, 165
Gordon, James, 71
Gordon, Sandy, 164, 165
Gordon & MacPhail, 87, 88
Goren, Tomer, 209
Gottlieb, Robert, 64
Grain whiskey, 185–186
GrandMetGuiness (GMG), 108
Grand Metropolitan, 107, 108
Grant, Ulysses, 98, 99–100
Grant, William, 164
   Stand Fast Blended Whisky of, 164
Great Northern Distillery, 177
Great Spirits, 160
Great Western Distillery, 113, 114–115
Green, George, 90
Green, Nathan, 90–91, 206
Green, Nearest, 73
Greenbrier Distillery, 149
Green Brier Tennessee Whiskey, 88
Green Chartreuse, 30–31
Greene, Heather, 12
Greenhut, Joseph, xiv, 113–114, 126
Grosser, Jeremy, 201
Guiness, xiv, 101, 107, 108
Guiness, Arthur, 54, 168
Guiness United Distillers, 109

Haga, Petrus de, as knight, 36
Haggart, Gary, 26
Haig, 37, 69, 78

as brand, 174, 196
DIMPL, 69
establishment of distilling dynasties, xii.
Haig, James, 69
Haig, John, 37, 52
Haig, Robert, 36, 52, 69
Haig, William, 69
Haig & Haig Blended Scotch Whisky, 69–70
Hale, Margaret Stein, 52
Hamilton, Alexander, 58, 128, 204
Hamilton, Ed, 43
Haner, Carl, 139
Hanyu Distillery, 210
Harper, L. W., 101
Harrison, William, 84–85
Hatch, Harry, 93, 141, 142, 149, 196
Hatch's Navy, 142
Hazelburn, 146
Heaven Hill Distillery, 57, 107, 137, 139
Hedonism, 186
Henderson, Lincoln, 207
Henry IV, King of England, 30
Henry VIII, King of England, 32, 37, 54
Hesing, Anton, 99
Heublein, Inc., xiv, 152
Hiram Walker, 88, 101, 149
   decanters of, 163
Hobart, 82
Hollow, Possum, Rye, 100
Hotaling, Anson Parsons, warehouse of, 134–135, 183
Hughes, Catherine, 206–207
Hughes, John Joseph, 206
Hughes, Michael, xii., 206
Hughes Bros. Distillers, xii
Hundred Years' War, xii
Hydrometer, 14–15
Hypatia, 14

Imperial Crown Whisky, 115, 192
Independent bottlers, 86–87
Indian-made foreign liquor (IMFL), 154

Index

Internal Revenue, Bureau of, 98–99
International Distillers and Vintners (IDV), 108, 109, 155
Inver House Scotch Whisky, 139
Irish Distillers Limited (HDL), xiv, 33, 167, 168, 176
Irish Famine, 124–125
Irish Whiskey, xv, 79, 168–169

Jackson, Michael, 24, 26
Jacob's Pardon, 173
Jagale, Rakshit, 155
Jagdale, Neelakanta "Neel," 154–155
Jagdale, Radhakrishna, 154
James I, King of England, 32
James IV, King of England, 24
Jameson, as Irish whiskey, 169, 176, 196, 206
Jameson, John, 39, 52, 54–55, 92, 205
Jameson, John, and son, 166, 167
Jameson, John, II, 53
Jameson, William, 39, 53, 92
Jameson's Bow Street Distillery, xiv, 168
James VI, King of Scotland, 32
Japanese whisky, xv
Jardine, Bruce, 184
Jefferson, Thomas, 60, 204, 205
Jenever, 18–19
Jim Beam. *See* Beam, Jim
JM Concepts, 201
Johnnie Walker, 62, 63, 164, 183, 185
John's Lane, 168
Johnson, Andrew, 98
Johnson, R. G., 101
Joseph, Bruce, 182
Judgment of Paris (1976), 152, 182
Justerini & Brooks (J&B), 108, 183

Kakubin, 147–148, 161
Kalkshtein, Gal, 208–209
Kavalan Single Malt Whisky, 197

Keepers of the Quaich, 34
Kehyari, Cyrus, xii., 206
Kennedy, Joe, 70
Kennetpans, 36, 78
Kentucky Distillers' Association, 128
Kentucky Straight Bourbon Whiskey, 85
Kerotakis device, 12
Kilbagie, 36, 78
Kilbeggan (blended Irish whiskey), 177
Kings County Distillery, 12
King Whisky blend, 161
Kirin
  agreement with Seagram, 174
  holdings of, 194–195
  Tanaka, John, and, 174–175
Knappogue Castle, 158–160
Knob Creek, 51
Knockdhu, 139
Koji process, 125–127
Kornschnappes, 42
Kotobukiya/Suntory, 146

Laboisier, Antoine, 76
Lamsden, Bill, 59
Laphroaig, 183
Lark, Bill, 82, 83
Lark, Lyn, 83
Lark Distillery, 83
Lawrenceburg Distillers Indiana (LDI), 205
Lee, Elmer T., 205
Lee, Hancock, 104
Leopold, Scott, 189
Leopold, Todd, 92, 188–189
Leopold Brothers, 116, 188
"Liberties," 37–38
Limerick Distillery, 124
Lincoln, Thomas, 51
Lincoln County Process, charcoal filtration used in, 72–73
Lindores Abbey Distillery, 24–26, 196
Linkwood Distillery, 65, 70
The Little Book of the Philosopher's Stone (book), 11
Lockhart, J., 163

Lot 40, 141
Louth, 177
Luxco, 205
Lynchburg, Virginia, 90

The Macallan (1928), 143–144, 183, 199
MacDonald, Andy, 186–187
Mackay, 79, 192, 202
Mackenzie Whisky, 94–95, 202
Macleod, Stephanie, 12
Magnus, Albertus, 10
Maker's Mark, 59
Mallya, Vijay, 202
Malt Riots, 70
Malt taxes, xii, 40, 64, 70–71
Malt whiskey, 19
Malt wine, 19
Manhattan Distillery, 126
Maria the Prophetess, 12
Maryland rye, 136–137
Mary's bath, 12–13
Mary the Jewess, 12
Maytag, Fritz, 182
McCarthy, Steve, 184
McDonald, John, 98, 99–100
McEwan, Jim, 192, 193
McGuane, Louise, 125
McKenna, Henry, 205
Mennonites, 44–45
Methanol, 38
Michter's Distillery, 44, 145, 146, 163
Middlings, 50
Midwest Grain Products (MGP), 173, 205
M&H Elements, 209
Milk & Honey, 196, 209
Mitchell, J. A., firm of, 87
Mitchell & Son, 88
Miyagikyo Distillery, 77, 147
Molasses, 42–43
Molasses Act (1733), 42
Molson, John, 80
Molson, Thomas, 80
Molson, William, 80
Molson Distillery, 79–80
Molson Golden, 80
Monongahela Mash, 61
Monongahela rye, 60

Monozukuri, 148
Moore, Thomas, 100
Moscow Mule, 153
Mountain dew, 42
Mulligan, Dave, 39

National, 101, 172
Nelson, Andrew, xiii, 89
Nelson, Charles, xiii, 88–89
Nelson Brothers Classic Bourbon, 89
Newman, Simon, 139
Nikka Whisky Distilling, xiv, 77, 145, 146, 160, 161, 163, 206, 210
Noe, Booker, 67
Nomad Outland Whisky, 95
North British Distillery Company, 78, 79

Oberholzer, Abraham, 60, 61
Oberholzer, Henrich, 60
Octomore, 193
OFC (Old Fired Copper or Old Fashioned Copper), 104, 122
Old Bushmills Whiskey, 32
Old Classic, 139
Old Crow Whiskey, 75
Old Duff Genever, 19
Old Fitzgerald Distillery, 107
Old Forester Bourbon, 118, 167
Old Fortuna, 106
Old Highland Whisky, 62
Old Judge Distillery, 107
Old Parr, 147, 164
Old Pepper Distillery, 74–75
Old Potrero, 183
Old Rip Van Winkle, 107, 170
Old Taylor Distillery, 121–122
Old Tub, 66–67
Old Vatted Glenlivet Whisky, 79
Ole Smokey Distillery, 201
Oloroso grapes, 143
Optic, 199
Overholts, 44, 60–61, 66, 205
Oxbridge, 199
Oxmoor Farm, 128, 129
Oxmoor Kentucky Whiskey, 129

Painter, John, 100
Palm Bay International, 173
Palmer, Elbridge, 106
Pappy Van Winkle, 170–171, 194, 205
    Family Reserve Kentucky Straight Bourbon Whiskey, 170–171
Old Rip Van Winkle, 107, 170
    Pappy Van Winkle's Family Reserve, 170–171, 194

Paris Wine Tasting (1976), 152
Patent medicines, 132
Paterson, Richard, 95, 202–203
Pattison, Robert and Walter, 164
Penderyn Distillery, 196, 198
Penn, William, 44
Pennco, 44
Pennsylvania rye, 60
Pepper, James E., xii, 61, 101, 103
Pepper, Oscar, 74, 75
Perry, Matthew (Commodore), 160
Peter the Great, 55
Phillips, Thomas, 32
Phylloxera, 79
Pickerell, Dave, 59
Pikesville Rye, 137
Pinch, 70
Poitín, xii, 32, 37–39, 40
Poke, Brian, 83
Poke, Fay, 83
Pontefract, James, 100–101
Port Charlotte, 193
Port Ellen, 65, 184, 192
Pot stills, 65
Power, James, 55, 118, 122–123
Power, John, 53
Powers Distillery, xiv, 39, 55, 118, 122–123, 159, 168, 176
Powers John's Lane Single Pot Still Irish Whiskey, 55
Presbyterianism, 32
Prichard, Benjamin, 73
Prohibition, xii, xiv, 33, 67, 82, 93, 101, 106, 129, 137, 142, 149, 152, 176, 204

Protestant Reformation, 44
Publicker, Harry, 137, 139
Pulteney, 139
Pure Food and Drug Act (1906), 41, 102, 128, 129, 133, 188, 207

Quaich, 34

Radico Khaitan, 154
Ramble Round the Globe, A (book), 120
Rebel Yell, 107
Redemption Rye, 61, 149
Repeal, 139
Reynier, Mark, 192–193
Reynier, Ruari, 192–193
Riachi, Roy, 212–213
Ricard, Pernod, xiv, 33, 97, 125, 141, 155, 167, 168, 169, 205
Riley, James, xv, 92
Riley Patent, 92
Rittenhouse, 139
River Spey, 60
Robinson, Maureen, 185
Rockefeller, John D, Standard Oil owned by, 126
Rockefeller, John D., John D's ownership of, 126
Roe, Peter, 39, 53, 54, 167
Roper, Lisa, 59
Rosenbloom, Sol, 101
Rosenstiel, Lewis, 101, 149, 174
Ross, George, 204
Ross & Squibb
    distillery owned by, 205
    warehouse owned by, 173
Rossville Distillery, 204
Royal Stag, 154–155
Royal Welsh Whisky, 198
Rozelieures Distillery, 179
Rum, 42
Rumbullion, 42
Russell, Jimmy, 59, 205
Rutlege, Jim, 174–175
Rye
    Belle of Bedford Straight, 206
    Monongahela, 60
    Pennsylvania, 60

Rye (*continued*)
   Pikesville, 137
   Redemption, 61, 149
   Stauning Floor Malted, 116
   three-Chamber, 189

Saladin, Charles, xiii, 115–116
Saluzzo, Angelo, 76
Sanderson, William, xiii., 78, 94
Sazerac, xiv, 101, 105, 107, 115
Schenks Homestead, 44, 66
Schenley Distillery, xiv, 60, 101, 103, 172, 174
Schmier, Dave, 205
Scotch whiskey, xv, 183, 184
   Dewar, 160, 162, 174, 183, 185
   regulations of, 68
Scotland, Duties on Spirits Act (1814) in, 71
Scotland and Its Whiskies (book), 24
Scottish Distillers Association, 69
Seagram, Edward, 113
Seagram, Joseph, xiii, 33, 52, 101, 112, 113
   Flour Mill and Distillery Company, 112
   VO Canadian, 112, 113
Seagram, Thomas, 33, 113
Seagram's, 92, 113, 172, 194, 195, 205
   agreement with Kirin, 174
   blended Crown Royal, 149, 151
   decanters of, 163
   legacy of, 174–175
   Suncoast of, 152
Settsu Shuzo, 144–145
Shackleton, Ernest, 202–203
Shannon Estuary, 124
Shell and tube condenser, 48, 50
Shenk, John, 44–45
Sherman Antitrust Act (1890), 126
Shinozaki Brewery and Distillery, 126
Shirakawa Distillery, 160–161
Shuzo, Settsu, 146

Single malts, coming to America, 183–184
Single Malt Scotch Whisky, 186
Single Pot Still Whiskey, 54
Smirnoff Vodka, xiv, 152–153
Smith, Andrew McKenzie, 24, 26
Smith, George, 67, 71, 78
Smith, McKenzie, 26
Smuggling, 28–29
Solimant, Laurent, 76
Somerset Imports, 70
Soule, Asa, 132
Sour mash, 74–75
Speyburn, 139
Spirit, 11
Spirits Safe, 64–65
Springbank Distillery, 87, 116, 146
Squibb, W. P., 101, 204
St. Bernard of Abbeville, 24
Stagg, George, 101, 104, 121–122, 133
Stand Fast Blended Whisky, 164–165
Starwood Nova, 83
Stauning Distillery, 116
Stauning Floor Malted Rye, 116
Stein, Andrew, 36
Stein, John, 36
Stein, Margaret, 37
Stein, Robert, 37, 76–77, 78
Steins, 36, 37, 69, 78
   establishment of distilling dynasties under, xii.
Still, 50
Stitzel, Arthur Phillip, 103, 106, 107, 170
Stitzel Weller Distillery, 106, 107, 139, 163, 170
Striding Man, 62
Sugar Act (1764), 42
Suntory, 67, 141, 146, 160, 161, 177, 184, 206, 210
   Suntory Global Spirits, 51
   Suntory Whisky, 145, 146, 148
Sutton, Marvin "Popcorn," 200–201
Swan, Jim, 26, 196–197, 198, 209

Taft, William, 128, 129, 172
Takamine, Jobichi, xiii, 114, 125–126
Takara Shuzo Co., 161
Taketsuru, Masataka, xiv, 77, 144–145, 160, 196
Taketsuru Pure Malt, 147
Talisker, 63, 186–187
Tanaka, 175
Tandhu, 116
Tasmania, 82–83
Tatlock & Thomson, 196
Taxes
   excise, 41, 70
   under Lincoln, Abraham, xii
   malt, xii, 40, 64, 70–74
   whiskey, xii, 40–41, 66, 89
Taylor, E. H., 74, 102, 104, 105
Taylor, E. H., Jr., 121–122, 128
Taylor, Mamie, 153
Teacher, Adam, 140
Teacher, Agnes Bergius, 140–141
Teacher, William, xv, 140
Teacher's, 185
   Highland Cream Scotch Whisky, 140–141
   self-opening bottle of, 162
Teeling, John, xiv, 176–177, 184
Teeling, Walter, 55, 176
Teeling Distillery, 177
Temperance movement, xiii–xix, 82
Ten High Sour Mash, 115
Tennessee White Whiskey, 201
Thomand Gate, 124
Thomas, Jerry, 19
Three-Chamber Rye Whiskey, 189
Tironensian Order, 24
Tolman, L. N., 188
Torii, Shinjiro, xiv, 144, 145, 146, 147–148, 160, 184
Torii Shoten (Suntory), 88, 147
Tullamore DEW, 12, 159

Uisce beatha, 33, 37, 44, 54, 84
United Distillers, 101, 107, 108, 109
United Distillers and Vintners (UDV), 109

Usher, Andrew, 78, 79
Usher, John, 78, 79
Usher's, 141, 160
    Green Label, 147
    Old Vatted Glenlivet Whiskey, 78–79

Van Buren, Martin, 84
Van Diemen's Land, 82
Van Winkle, Julian, III, 170
Van Winkle, Julian, Jr., 106, 107, 170
Van Winkle, Julian "Pappy," 106, 107, 139, 170–171, 205
Vat 69, 78, 94–95, 185
Vendome Works, 188–189
Vintners Scotland, 109
Vital du Four, 21, 132
Vitale, David, 83
Vodka, 152–153
Volstead Act, 102–103, 142

Walker, Alexander, 62, 63, 162
Walker, Emma, 12, 63
Walker, Hiram, xiii, 79, 80, 92, 93, 95–97, 101, 114–115, 141, 149, 163, 205
Walker, John, 68, 88, 170, 205
Walkerville, 96–97
Wallace, William, 36

Warenghem, Léon, 178, 184
Warner, H. H., 132
Wash Act (1784), 64, 79
Washington, George, 58–59
Wasmund, Rick, 208
Watson, John, 78
WB Breton whiskey, 179
Weaver, Fawn, 90–91
Weller, William, 106, 107, 170
Welsh Wind, 198
Whiskey backstory, 51
Whiskey Breton, 179
Whiskey Excise Tax (1701), 128
Whiskey Rebellion (1792), 71, 182
Whiskey Ring, 98, 99
Whiskey Row, 56
Whiskey Trust, xiii, xiv, 113–115., 126
Whiskey/whisky
    Canadian, xv
    controversy over spelling of, xv
    French, 178–179
    grain, 185–186
    Indian, 153–155
    Irish, xv, 79, 168–169
    Japanese, xv
    pure malt, 132–133
    rye, 44, 60–61

    Scotch, xv, 68, 183, 184
    segmenting in Japan, 160–161
    white, xiv, 79, 168–169
Whyte, 192, 202
Wicker, Lisa, 12
Widow Jane, 59
Wild Turkey, 59
William, Duke of Normandy, 36
Williams, Evan, 56–57, 197–198, 206
Willowbank Distillery, 174
Wilson, Andrea, 12
Wiser, J. P., 80, 92, 205
    distillery of, 141
Women's Christian Temperance Union (WCTU), 82
Woodford Reserve, 208
Worm tub, 48–50
Worts, James, 92
Woulfe, Peter, 76

Ximénez, Pedro, grapes of, 143

Yamazaki Distillery, 145, 146, 161, 184
Yoichi Distillery, 146–147

Zosimos of Panopolis, 10, 12

Photo by: Amy Dudash Robinson

ROBIN ROBINSON is the author of *The Complete Whiskey Course*, named a *Whisky Advocate* Must-Read Book and a Tales of the Cocktail Best New Book, among other accolades. A renowned whiskey educator, noted judge on evaluation panels, and private consultant to the spirits industry, he received the Icon of Whisky Award from *Whisky Magazine*, their highest commendation for brand ambassadors. He created the popular Whiskey Smackdown tasting series at Astor Center in New York City; has taught at the Culinary Institute of America and Moonshine University; and has presented at the American Distilling Institute, Bar Institute, and elsewhere. He lives in New Jersey.